INDIA'S FIGHTERS

INDIA'S FIGHTERS: THEIR METTLE, HISTORY AND SERVICES TO BRITAIN.

SAINT NIHAL SINGH

ILLUSTRATED

GYAN

Published by

Gyan Publishing House
5, Ansari Road
Daryaganj, New Delhi-110002
Phone: 011-47034999, 9811692060
E-mail: books@gyanbooks.com

Distribution Network
gyanbooks.com
India, USA, Canada, UK, Australia, France

ISBN : 978-81-212-9534-5 (PB)
First Published, 1914

2nd Impression 2023

Printed at: Gyan Press, Delhi.

INDIA'S FIGHTERS
Author: SAINT NIHAL SINGH

Photo by G. T. Jones & Son, Kingston-on-Thames.

SIKH OFFICERS OF THE VICEROY'S BODYGUARD.

INDIA'S FIGHTERS: THEIR METTLE, HISTORY AND SERVICES TO BRITAIN.

BY

SAINT NIHAL SINGH,

Author of "India's Fighting Troops," "Progressive British India," "Japan's Modernization," "Urge Divine," "Glimpses of the Orient To-day," "Making Bad Children Good," "Messages of Uplift for India," "Essays on India," Etc., Etc.

ILLUSTRATED.

1914.

TO

MY FATHER,

BIJAI NIHAL SINGH,

I DEDICATE THIS BOOK AS A SLIGHT TOKEN OF MY LOVE FOR HIM AND MY ADMIRATION FOR HIS INVINCIBLE SPIRIT, AND HIS LEARNING AND PIETY.

THE AUTHOR.

LITERARY CONTENTS.

PICTORIAL CONTENTS.

EXPLANATORY NOTE.

This little volume aims at giving a bird's-eye view of India's fighting clans—their origin, their deeds of dash and daring, their past services to Britain, and their part in the Armies of British India and of the Rajas.

It makes no pretensions to being an exhaustive study of the organisation of the armies of India, or a complete history of their growth and accomplishments. Apart from the limitations of space and time at my disposal, my design has not been to essay such tasks. On the contrary, I have endeavoured to give a general idea of the extent and quality of Hindostan's military resources, and thereby supply a lack which has impressed many as unfortunate in the interests of the British Empire, the Oriental Dependency, and the world at large.

The account I supply here is a plain, unvarnished tale, free from hyperbole. Yet

I write as one descended from fighting stock —one who justifiably glories in the heroism and faithfulness of his people.

I have striven hard to rule technicalities out of the work. I have even prevailed upon myself to employ Indian terms whose spelling outrages me, just because they have been adopted by the British Army authorities. But freedom from technicalities and pedantry should not be taken to imply that I have not done my best to make the book reliable. Slight as the volume is, it has required considerable research work, of which the many references to authorities give some idea. I freely acknowledge my indebtedness to the regimental histories, etc., consulted by me.

The book as it stands has been especially written for the present occasion. I have contributed, during this year, to British, American, and Indian publications, many articles dealing with various phases of the subject. Though I had full option to make use of this matter—thanks to the courtesy of the many editors for whom the articles were written—yet the scheme of this work did not permit of my availing myself of this privilege to any appreciable extent, and what appears within these covers has all been re-written.

I owe grateful thanks for invaluable help rendered me in the collection of the material, in giving it the form in which it now appears, and in revising proofs, to Cathleyne Saint Nihal Singh, my wife and colleague.

I am also indebted to General Sir Edmund George Barrow, G.C.B., Military Secretary, India Office; Sir T. W. Holderness, K.C.S.I., I.C.S., B.A., Under Secretary of State for India; Lieut.-Colonel Sir James R. Dunlop-Smith, K.C.S.I., C.I.E., Political Aide-de-Camp to the Secretary of State for India; W. Foster, Esq., C.I.E., Registrar and Superintendent of Records, India Office; and Dr. F. W. Thomas, M.A., Librarian, India Office, for the opportunities afforded me for obtaining necessary information.

I express my obligation to his Highness

the Maharaja-Gaekwar of Baroda, Shri Sir Sayaji Rao III., Gaekwar, G.C.S.I.; his Highness the Thakore Sahib of Gondal, Shri Sir Bhagvat Sinhji, G.C.I.E.; Captain the Honourable Malik Umar Hayat Khan Tiwana, C.I.E., M.V.O., and Messrs. George T. Jones and Son, of Kingston-on-Thames, for the photographs which they supplied me; and to the publishers for supplementing these pictures with prints they secured locally.

I highly esteem the courtesy of Messrs. Sampson Low, Marston and Co., in giving their consent to my writing a brochure on "India's Fighting Troops," for Messrs. George Newnes, Ltd.; and of the latter firm for leaving me unfettered in respect of copyright and other considerations, to prepare the present work.

SAINT NIHAL SINGH.

46, Overhill Road, East Dulwich,
London, S.E., England,
December, 1914.

INDIA'S FIGHTERS.

CHAPTER I.

The Mettle of the Men.

I WRITE of India's fighters, who, in 1914, for the first time in history are waging war on European soil, but who, in the past, have often rushed to the firing line to help to crush Britain's enemies—European, African, and Asiatic—and who have fought many times to establish, consolidate, and save the British dominion in Hindostan, and to assist in conserving Imperial interests in many parts of Asia and Africa.

Men of valorous deeds, their heroism and chivalry are writ large in the annals of Ind from the dim dawn of civilization down to our day and age. Men of soldierly tribes, they have fought under many standards, and with varying success, but never have they hesitated to pour out their blood when duty called them to face their own or their Suzerain's enemies; nor have they ever turned their back upon unconquered foes.

A multitude of races are they, with a mixture of blood flowing in their veins. The aboriginal stock of the Peninsula, crossed by numerous foreign strains and subjected to the climatic influences of the country, which range between frigid and tropical, has produced a congeries of people with distinctive physiques, features, and temperaments, each with its own traditions and civilization, each with its own pantheon of gods and goddesses, each with its own interests and affinities.

Among them are tall men, some of whom are slender and some heavy set, and others of medium height and build. Others, again, are short and slim, or, in some cases, stout. Some carry themselves majestically, others do not have a military bearing. All are good fighters, no matter what their figures may be.

Some men among them have coal-black locks, black eyes, and very dark skins. Others have a brownish complexion—"the colour of wheat," as the Indians describe it—and dark brown hair and eyes. Still others have fair skin, light hair, and blue or grey eyes.

Some of the men have regular, clean-cut features—oval faces, with high, expansive foreheads, eyes almond-shaped and set wide apart, large, straight noses, small mouths and firm chins—and are so handsome that they are admired by all who look at them. Others have faces so irregular—with oblique eyes and high cheekbones and a yellowish complexion—that their only charm lies in the courage and strength of character that is stamped upon their every lineament. Among them are a few whose countenances are neither beautiful nor expressive of character. They have pointed faces, with low, narrow foreheads, prominent cheek bones, thick lips, and small chins. But all can give a good account of themselves on the battlefield.

Some of them are soft-spoken men with a kind expression. It is hard to irritate them, and they are always well-mannered, in peace or in war, in regimental line or in the drawing room. Others have terrifying, awe-inspiring looks, and their eyes flash fire and their faces redden at the least provocation. Others again are haughty looking men, whose every feature and every movement bespeak their belief that they are born to dominate.

Some of India's fighters totally abstain from liquor, others will drink anything in the shape of spirits, wine, and beer, whether it be country-brewed or foreign, and will consume an amazing quantity of it without showing intoxication. Some consider it the greatest sin to smoke. Others eat opium, and several clans are addicted to the use of tobacco and drugs. Some will not eat meat of any kind, others will eat anything, even snakes, worms, and carrion. The meat eaters are fastidious in the extreme. Some refuse beef altogether. Some will not eat pork. Others will not eat the flesh of an animal that has not been killed by a single stroke, while certain among them demand that the beast must have its throat slit while set formulas are being muttered aloud. Rice is the staff of life of some, wheat of others. Some do not care who cooks or hands them their food. Others require their meals to be prepared and served by people of approved birth. Whatever their habit or belief may be, they usually cast their prejudices to the four winds when engaged on the battlefield and let nothing mar their usefulness as soldiers.

In intelligence they vary as greatly as they do in other matters. Some are sharp-witted. Others are slow of understanding. Some readily learn to read and write and are apt at mastering foreign languages. Others are just the reverse. Only a small percentage of them are literate. Not a few look upon literacy as a sign of effeminacy, and hold *literati* in contempt. But they are not ignorant, by any means. Of epic literature many of them know much. Manly traditions have descended to them from generation to generation, and they are all repositories of tales of the exploits of their clansmen, some of which are real, though more or less glorified, while many of them are out and out legends.

In moral and spiritual qualities they represent civilizations poles apart. Some hold personal virtue dearer than the breath of their life, and are strictly monogamous. Others include polygamy as a tenet of their creed, though few actually practise it. Truthfulness, honesty, and cleanliness they, with few exceptions, value highly. Some worship God, One and Indivisible, Self-created and Creator of all, All-seeing, All-hearing, All-powerful, in

Whom, in course of time, their personality must merge, which state they regard as salvation, to be attained by a life of piety and devotion, and not by intercession. Others pin their faith to God, Omnipotent and All-merciful, Whom they can reach only through the mediation of His chosen Prophet. Others worship the Creative, Destructive, and Protective Elements of nature, associating one or more of these principles with half-human, half-divine personalities who are regarded as the incarnation of God in His various aspects. Oriental imagination, running riot, has produced a pantheon whose deities are said to outnumber the total population of India—some three hundred and fifteen odd millions. The incarnations are female and male, often paired together, and sometimes with children, the remarkable thing about the family being that the name of the goddess precedes that of the god. To the initiated, the images that are made to represent the deities have deep symbolical meaning; but to the uninitiated some appear to be grotesque and a few barbaric. For instance, one of them is depicted as a female with a face as black as coal and grinning mouth, her locks in disarray, wearing around her neck a garland of human skulls, dripping with blood. Some do not require images for their worship, but bow to natural phenomena, such as lightning, streams, mountains, the sun, and fire.

But short or tall, black or fair-skinned, handsome or homely, intelligent or slow-witted, idol-breaker or image-worshipper, all of them know how to handle arms with deadly effect. At various stages of India's development, its fighters have wielded weapons of diverse descriptions. In the infancy of the world they used bows and wooden arrows. Afterwards iron arrows were substituted. The dagger, sword, and lance were employed later, and the warriors used their shields and wore armour of burnished steel or chain to defend themselves against the death-dealing thrusts of their foes. Later still muskets and guns

A GROUP OF GURKHA INFANTRYMEN.

came into use. After Hindostan's contact with the West, breech-loaders of various patterns were employed, one succeeding the other, until to-day the fighters of India are armed with rifles of the most modern type. Whatever their arms, the Indians have always used them with the greatest skill. The arrow and the bullet have always gone straight to their mark. The sword and the bayonet, the dagger and the lance, have been plunged deep into the flesh of their foes. Even when fighting enemies with superior arms, the Indian clansmen with their primitive weapons have given a good account of themselves. With surprising agility the Indians have cast aside their own methods of warfare and taken up the arms and military tactics of Europe; and they have acquired an efficiency in handling the new weapons which has won the admiration of friends and foes alike.

Certain qualities are common to them all. They will fight to the finish and die rather than turn their backs on an unbeaten foe. They will be docile and affectionate to those who are placed in authority over them and who, by bravery, kindness, consideration, and justice have won their regard. They will never shirk the call of duty. They will bear without complaint extremes of heat and cold. They will unmurmuringly suffer hunger and thirst. Mountains and jungles, rivers and deserts, have no terrors for them. Whether they are well or ill-paid, whether they have a hard or an easy time of it, they will be soldiers if they possibly can. The only other profession beside that of bearing arms which many of them look upon with favour is that of a ruler.

Administration and militarism still go hand in hand in the Indian imagination. The overwhelming majority of the close upon seven hundred Rajas who govern territories of varying dimensions, thinly or thickly populated, rich or poor in resources, are the lineal descendants of men who carved out kingdoms with their sharp and trusty swords. The military spirit still burns brightly in not a few of them. There are among them Rajas with grey heads, whose only passion is to die fighting. Others there are, not yet out of their teens, who will not be denied the privilege of battling for the right. Leading their cavalry, camelry, and infantry in times of war, and riding over the roughest kind of ground and hunting dangerous game in times of peace, appeal to them as does nothing else. They have fought for the British on numerous occasions, and will fight for them as many times again, if need be.

Of high or humble rank, Raja or commoner, the Indian fighters have established a record of which the warriors of any nation might well be proud. Their exploits stretch back far beyond the time when history began, to the misty morn of romance and chivalry, and are sung in epics of indescribable pathos and beauty. Traditions of warriors who lived and fought and nobly died in early and mediaeval periods could be related by the thousand, but I shall content myself with describing a few of the gallant deeds of Indian soldiers during recent years, when fighting for the British Empire, to show the type of manhood which, for the first time, is engaged in combat with Great Britain's European enemies on European soil. This I do in Chapter IV., after describing the fighting clans, and their part in the Indian Armies in the two chapters that immediately follow.

CHAPTER II.

Fighting Clans.

AT various periods of human history, waves of fiery races have surged into India from its north-west corner, submerging everything that came in their way. In the course of centuries these peoples have intermingled with one another and with Hindostan's aborigines. This amalgamation of widely differing social elements, subjected to the bitter cold and hardy mountain life of the north, the broiling sun of the belt of the Peninsula, and the humid heat of the south, has produced clans and tribes who vary greatly in face, form, and manly qualities, whose number is legion. From the point of view of fighting, many of them have no value whatever, and others are indifferent material;

but several have managed to retain, to a surprising extent, the martial qualities which made their ancestors famous. I am not concerned here with any but the virile population of Hindostan; but to understand its composition it is necessary to turn the pages of the annals of the land backwards, and note how the important waves of immigrants flowed successively into the country and became absorbed by it.

Travelling back to the time when tradition daubs patches of gaudy colours upon the dense darkness of days beyond human ken, the student of prehistoric periods discovers caravans of fair-skinned people with regular features migrating into what is now Afghanistan and contiguous regions and crossing the ranges of Hindu Kush into the rich, fertile plains of what is to-day the Punjab, drained by many rivers. Whence they came is a moot question which still remains definitely to be settled. One theory, recently put forward has it that their home was in the north of Europe, within full sight of the Aurora Borealis.[1] The older conjecture is that they had their origin in the highlands of central Asia—the region bordering the banks of the Oxus. There are many other guesses current, hotly pressed by protagonists, and fiercely denounced by antagonists. The reasons for and against these hypotheses cannot be stated here; but in any case it is believed that streams of human beings poured out in all directions from a common centre, some peopling the different countries of Europe, others making their way to Persia, Afghanistan, India, etc.

In view of the fact that in the year 1914 Indians were engaged in fighting Germans on European soil, it may be parenthetically mentioned that certain authorities consider that the two peoples are descended from the same parent stock. Peschel, quoted by Sir Herbert Risley in *The People of India*, p. 24, "divides the Caucasian type into (*a*) Indo-

1. *The Arctic Home of the Vedas*, by Bal Gangadhar Tilak.

Germans, (*b*) Semites, (*c*) Hamites or Barbers, and includes the 'Hindus' (non-Dravidian Indians) in the first of these groups."

Aside from these theories, there is one which asserts that the Aryans did not migrate into the Peninsula, but originated there. This is, in many ways, the most unsatisfactory of the contentions raging in regard to this question. I, therefore, adhere to the view that, early in human history, large tribes of Aryans moved from their joint home in various directions, one of them coming to India.

The Indian branch of these immigrants called themselves Aryans—the noble—a term which is now applied to the whole race. Another branch of the same ethnical group which settled in Persia called the Indian settlers "Hindus," meaning "thieves"—an appellation which shows the contempt of the Perso-Aryans for the Indo-Aryans. It appears that the two clans had quarrelled with each other and left their homeland in different directions. That they entertained violent enmity towards each other is evidenced by the fact that Indian terms which are perfectly proper are opprobrious expressions in Persian, and *vice versâ*. Some claim that the Indo-Aryans were called Hindus because they made their homes on the banks of the Indus. But if that is the case, how did the river get this name? The question naturally rises, was it styled thus to designate it as the thieves' (Hindus') river? And was the mountain-chain in the north-west of India, which the Indo-Aryans crossed to enter the Peninsula, called Hindu Kush, or "thieves' mountain" (*Kush* being a corruption of the Persian word *Koh*, meaning a high elevation)? Or did the Perso-Aryans give it that name to imply that the mountain might prove the death of the "thieves" (Indo-Aryans), *Kush*, in Persian, meaning killed? According to other authorities, the term Hindu was first used in connection with the Indo-Aryans by another wave of immigrants which originated in Arabia, and of which I speak later. Be this as it may, the word has been applied for centuries, and still is given to this race which settled in India in the early dawn of human civilization, and to other peoples whom it included within its fold.

From what is known of them they well deserved the name—Aryan, or noble—which they had chosen for themselves. They led a simple, pastoral life, highly valued purity of conduct, placed spiritual welfare above worldly wealth, loved poetry, and composed and sang lofty hymns. They held in reverence such elements of nature as the sun and fire. These they worshipped as symbols of creative energy, instead of prostrating themselves unthinkingly before them, as did the savages, who, struck dumb by natural phenomena, made fetiches of them.

They were not mere poets and dreamers, but were sturdy fighters, who displaced the natives of the countries to which they migrated. In India they came across people dark of skin and irregular of feature, believed to have belonged to the Dravidian race, who are believed to have originated in the Peninsula, but may have been immigrants.

In the course of a few centuries the Aryans settled in the country drained by the many rivers of the Punjab—including one, the Sarasvati, which has now disappeared. Later, some of them pushed into the valleys of the Jumna and Ganges, and their tributaries.

Two theories are current regarding the movement of the Indo-Aryans towards the east. One of them ascribes it to the growth of the immigrant population settled in the Punjab. The other suggests that a fresh wave of Aryans swept from the north-west down to the Gangetic plain (the *Madhya Desa*, or middle land of Hindu literature).

Some of the peoples whom the Aryans vanquished were driven into the mountain fastnesses and primeval forests of northern

India, while others crossed the Vindhya Hills, which formed the base of the triangle with the southern point of the Peninsula as its apex. Not a few of the Aborigines were so crushed in spirit that they consented to live in the land appropriated by the triumphant immigrants which the victors had named after themselves, "*Aryavarta*"[2] (the land of the Aryas, or noble men) on the most humiliating terms. These conquered people were set to work at employments in which the conquerors considered it beneath their dignity to engage. The victors reserved to themselves the privilege of forming connections, legal or "left-handed," mostly the latter, with the women of the vanquished race. But the aborigines and the progeny of mixed marriages could not aspire to marrying fair-skinned maidens,

2. This region is also known as Hindustan or Hindostan or the land (*sthan*) of the Hindus. I must make it clear that, used in this sense, Hindustan means only upper India, which at first was colonized by the Aryans. It does not include the triangular tract bounded on the north by the Vindhya hills. The term is, however, also employed in the general sense, as referring to the whole Peninsula. This use is of comparatively recent origin.

much less to have any illegal association with them. The dark-skinned people, full-blooded and half-castes alike, were denied all social intercourse with the ruling race and had no mission, and could have none, other than to cater for the pleasure of the Aryans. Such was the arrogance of the white to the black, of the victor to the vanquished, at the beginning of human history!

Degraded though the position of the aborigines was, it is to be noted that mixture of Aryan and autochthonous stock commenced in India very soon after the immigrants had possessed themselves of *Aryavarta*. In the course of centuries, this blending of race was destined to exert a profound influence upon the inhabitants of India.

The theorists who propound that a fresh wave of Indo-Aryans surged into the Gangetic region further contend that the new immigrants, unlike those who had preceded them, came without their women-folk, and, therefore, were compelled to content themselves with the native women of the conquered race. Those who thus speculate—and among their ranks are Dr. Hoernle, Dr. Grierson, and the late Sir Herbert H. Risley—affirm that this difference has had a far-reaching effect upon Indian ethnography, which may be thus summarized:

Owing to the fact that the Aryans who settled in the Punjab brought their women with them, they kept their racial purity, and, therefore, their descendants (principally Rajputs and Jats) approximate closely to the Aryan type—"a relatively long (dolichocephalic) head; a straight, finely-cut (leptorrhine) nose; a long, symmetrically narrow face; a well-developed forehead, regular features, and a high facial angle" (to use Sir Herbert Risley's words, extracted from pp. 47, 48 of his *The People of India*).

Since the Aryans who established themselves on the Gangetic plains had to take aboriginal women to be their wives, the people inhabiting parts of the United Provinces of

Agra and Oudh, Behar, and Orissa are not Aryans, though most of them have more or less admixture of Aryan blood. This intermixture led to the Aryan faith becoming gross, on account of the inclusion in it of the cruder notions and objects of worship of the aborigines.

Controversies will continue to rage about the way in which the racial mixture occurred. Therefore, I may continue to deal with the further progress of the Aryans.

For a considerable time the Aryan wave was checked by the Vindhya Hills. But the religious lore of the Hindus, ascribed to about the 7th century B.C., chronicles the poetic injunction of the sage Agastaya to this mountain "not to grow so high," and somewhere about that time the Aryans are believed to have braved the heights and crossed over into the land which they then designated as *Dakshina* (to the south), later vulgarized into *Dakkhan*, and still later into *Deccan*. Pressure exerted by the growth of population and a spirit of adventure seem to have caused this movement.

The Aryans found the people beyond the Vindhya Hills, also supposed to be of Dravidian race, much farther advanced and much more manly than the natives whom they had subjugated in northern India. The invaders prevailed in the end, but their supremacy was dearly bought.

The conquest of the Deccan and settlement among the Dravidians led the Aryans to incorporate into their religion many of the practices and rites of the conquered. Social ideals also changed, and much mixture of blood resulted. The intellectual life of the victors was considerably affected. Their language—Sanskrit—lost its pristine purity, had to admit numerous aboriginal terms, and became transformed when spoken by the original inhabitants of the country and the half-breeds. From this blending of the fair and dark-skinned races originated a civilization and people different from those in the

Punjab—and some of these variations have continued, in a more or less pronounced degree, to this generation.

While the Aryans were thus establishing themselves in the Peninsula, their society was undergoing rapid changes. At first they appear to have led a patriarchal life, each clan being headed by the pater familias (*Maha Raja*, as he was called), who presided over its temporal and spiritual affairs. Each clansman helped to produce food, and fought, when occasion arose, to protect the commonweal. No fixed lines of division of labour or social gradations then existed among the immigrant population.

As conditions settled, and Aryans reduced the aborigines to the condition of serfs and forced them to do hard and unpleasant tasks, the polity split into four occupational groups,[3] namely:

3. The Western world designates this classification as the "caste system." The word "caste" is derived from a

1. The Brahman or priestly and learned class, the members of which concerned themselves with mastering the religious literature which was handed down orally from one generation to another; and who learned to perform the rites that grew more and more elaborate as the decades passed by.

2. The Kshatriyas, later corrupted into Shatri, Khattri, and Chattri, or fighters and rulers, who undertook to protect and administer the affairs of the land which had been acquired, and to make additions to it by the strength of their arm.

3. The Vaishas, who engaged in economic pursuits of various kinds, trading,

---

Portuguese term, *casta*, meaning "the family." *Castus*, in Latin, signifies purity of breed. "Caste" does not accurately describe the institution, but is retained in this book in view of the currency it has acquired. I have not the space to trace the causes and course of its evolution. The Sanskrit term *varna* (colour) offers the key to its origin, namely, it had its beginning in the attempt to keep the whites (Aryans) and blacks (non-Aryan Indians) apart. This much appears to be indisputable. Later, however, the Aryans, semi-Aryans, and non-Aryans appear to have divided into occupational groups, to which reference is made above.

farming, etc., that were not deemed beneath the dignity of an Aryan to perform.

4. The Shudras, later corrupted into Sudras—menials, who engaged in work that was considered unfit for any "decent" human being to perform, and served the three higher castes. This order was composed of Dravidians and half-castes, and Aryans who had been degraded for heinous offences to this, the lowest station of life.

The priestly, military, and trading classes called themselves twice-born, because, as the males grew out of infancy, they were invested with the "sacred thread" or *yag-o-pveet*, a ceremony which marked their formal entrance into the society of noble or Aryan people, and was deemed their second birth. No Shudra might aspire to this dignity.

At first the higher castes were not kept strictly separated; but long before the beginning of the Christian era they became absolutely distinct from one another. Thenceforward men born in one or the other of these divisions remained in the group in which they first saw the light of day, and took up hereditary occupations. As the centuries passed by, the regulations became so rigid that, for instance, Kshatriyas were completely barred from becoming Brahams, etc.

The fourth division had, from the beginning, remained a section of society by itself, except for the privilege its women possessed of producing half-castes. But a few Shudras displayed such learning and piety that even the hardest-hearted of the Aryans could not deny them the homage that was their due, and venerated them even above Brahams. However, these exceptions were so rare that tradition has preserved them as unusual instances.

Long before the beginning of the first century, A.D., each of the four castes had split into many subdivisions. As the years raced by, this tendency to subdivide became accentuated, and in course of time Aryan, or Hindu, society became divided into

Photos by Stuart.

A Rajput Fighter.

A Mopila Soldier.

thousands upon thousands of sub-castes.

I cannot pursue this interesting subject to the point to which I should like to follow it, but I may say that many of the sub-castes appear to be tribes under a different name which wanted to preserve their separate entities. I may also add that the Hindus, early in their history, evolved the idea of trade-unionism, sub-castes becoming the shields which they used to hold off outsiders.

This book is chiefly concerned with the Kshatriya, or military caste, many clans of which have continued to retain their manhood, and constitute the back-bone of India's martial population. People belonging to this class, or at least some of them, have been known from the earliest times as Rajputs or "Rajas' (kings') sons," since they were administrators as well as fighters. The Rajputs have always ruled in some part or other of India and have ever been famous for their military mettle. Indian annals are full of their exploits. They have succeeded in preserving their characteristics through the ages. I shall have more to say of them later.

Though fighting was considered to be the special privilege of the Kshatriyas, yet other classes have engaged in soldiering, even after caste distinctions had grown very rigid and men were not allowed to assume occupations to which they had not been born. Among those who took up the profession of arms, but were not qualified by heredity to do so, were the Brahmans. The reasons assigned for this departure is that these men, pushed out of the priestly ranks by the rapid multiplication of their numbers, took to agriculture to support themselves, and learned the use of weapons in order to be able to defend their holdings and lives. A few of these Brahman castes continue to be virile, and contribute splendid soldiers to the armies of India.

Before I deal further with these Hindu martial races, I must take into account the other waves of immigration which swept into

Hindostan subsequent to the Aryan invasion, and introduced new racial elements.

About the second century B.C., Greeks began invading India. Alexander the Great, searching for new worlds to conquer, marched as far as the Indus, engaged in battle with a Rajput king whom the Greek historians designate as Porus, and defeated him. He moved eastward to the left bank of the Bias and achieved another great victory. He wanted to push his legions onwards towards the rising sun, but they refused to go any further, and he was forced to turn back to Macedonia.

During the 2nd and 1st centuries B.C., waves of Greeks from Bactria were literally crowded out of their homes and driven to India by a warlike tribe which originated in Scythia, the region round about the Black Sea. According to a more modern, and, I believe, more authentic account, this fierce race came, in the first instance, from southern China, and was called the Sse by the Chinese.

The Sse did not leave its home of its own free will, but appears to have been driven out by an allied people known as Yuchi or Yueh-chi.

The Greeks occupied portions of the Punjab and Rajputana. Some of them appear to have gone as far east as Orissa. But their Empire was short-lived.

The Scythians were not left in peace in possession of their new territories by the Yuchi, who, themselves, had been dislodged from China by the Ephlathalites, better known as Huns, about the first century, A.D. They moved eastwards, and, in the course of a few decades, spread over Afghanistan, the North-West Provinces, Baluchistan, the Punjab, Rajputana, and a considerable portion of the Gangetic plains. Chief among the Scythian clans which migrated to India are known to have been the *Medii*, *Xanthii*, *Jatii*, and *Getae*, who conquered the inhabitants of the *Aryavarta* and for a short time completely dominated the Aryans.

During the middle of the 1st century B.C. the Yuchi, driven by the Huns, gradually worked their way into Afghanistan, and pressed south into portions of what now are known as the Punjab, Rajputana and Bombay Presidency. They came into conflict with the other Scythian tribes, but won out in the struggle, and established their power over a large area of Western India. In Hindu literature their Empire is called "*Kushana*"; and the people are styled *Shakas* (*Sakas*), *Turushkas*, and *Tokhdri*.

In the middle of the 5th century A.D. India experienced another invasion, this time of a Mongol race, the Huns. In about fifty years they had established their sway over a large portion of Upper India.

Controversies rage as to whether or not these Mongol races mixed with the Indo-Aryans. To state the two important contentions:

One theory is that they did. It attributes to this crossing the splendid mettle of such fighting clans as the Rajputs and Jats. The name Jat is said to be derived from that of the Scythian tribe *Jatii*. The name borne by the hardy Gujars, who are herdsmen by profession, and who continue still to furnish a few soldiers, is said to be the corruption of Yuchi. The *Handbooks for the Indian Army*[4] compiled under the orders of the Government of India, and published by the Superintendent of Government Printing, India, gives prominence to these hypotheses.

Another theory has it that the Rajputs and Jats have not any Scytho-Hun blood in them, but are pure Aryans. This claim is supported

4. Of these, the following have come to the notice of the writer: *Brahmans*, by Captain A. H. Bingley and Captain A. Nicholls. 1897. *Rajputs*, by Captain A. H. Bingley. 1898. *Sikhs*, by Captain A. H. Bingley, 1899. *Mappilas or Moplahs*, by Major P. Holland-Pryor. 1904. *Jats, Gujars, and Ahirs*, by Major A. H. Bingley. 1904. *Gurkhas*, by Lieut.-Colonel Eden Vansittart. 1906. *Marathas and Dekhani Musalmans*, by Major R. M. Betham. 1908. *Dogras*, by Captain A. H. Bingley. Revised by Major A. B. Longden. 1910. *Pathans*, by Major R. T. I. Ridgway. 1910. *The Fighting Races of India*, by P. D. Bonarjee (1889), may also be mentioned in connection with these handbooks.

by that eminent authority, the late Sir Herbert H. Risley.[5]

He is of the opinion that the Scythians became amalgamated with the Dravidians of south-western India, and produced the fighting clans of Marathas, etc. This is a mere conjecture. As Mr. E. A. Gait, I.C.S., who superintended the last (1911) Census operations in India, remarks, this view "has not yet gained general acceptance. According to Professor Haddon (*The Wanderings of Peoples*, page 27), the foreign element is Alpine, not Mongolian, and may be due to an immigration of which the history has not been written."[6]

Before continuing to discuss further waves of immigration, it is necessary to note that the centuries which witnessed so many incursions of warlike tribes upon the Indo-Aryan settlements saw the rise and fall of a great Indian religion—Buddhism. Its

5. *The People of India,* by Sir H. H. Risley, K.C.I.E., C.S.I., pp. 58, 59, etc.

6. *General Report of the Census of India, 1911,* p. 383.

founder, Gautama Buddha, was born about the middle of the sixth century, B.C., in the ruling family of Kapilavastu, in north-eastern India. He was not of the priestly order, but belonged to the fighting caste. He revolted against the division of Aryan society into a multitude of subdivisions, which separated man from man, incited a few to despise and hate many, and weakened the body politic. He also rebelled against the Brahmanical religion, which held elaborate ritual and ceremonials at a premium, but did not insist upon purity of life. He declared that righteousness of conduct alone could procure salvation (*nirvana*), which he defined as a state of cessation of the pains and miseries of terrestrial life—the extinction of desire itself.

The lofty ideals that Buddha set up readily appealed to the people at large, who were tired of Brahmanical pretensions, sanguinary sacrifices and formalism. The Scythian invaders also fell under the spell of Buddha. Within a short time of its promulgation, Buddhism had become the dominant religion of the land, totally eclipsing Brahmanism. By 200 B.C. it had been adopted as the State religion, which hastened its dissemination.

But the persistent Brahmans never gave up their cause as altogether lost. They astutely worked to regain their power. Gradually they induced the people to regard Buddhism as a part of Hinduism. They deified Buddha, and gave him a place in the Hindu pantheon in order to make his followers feel that their Teacher was being elevated to a high plane, which Hindu gods alone could occupy. By the 5th century A.D. these shrewd tactics had prevailed, and the compliments which the Brahmans had paid to Buddha had practically driven his religion out of the Peninsula. According to the last census, there are slightly less than 350,000 Buddhists, excluding Burma, which, in itself, has 10,384,579.

This meant that by the 5th century those

who inhabited India at that time, composed, as they were, of diverse racial elements—of Aryan, Greek, Scythian, Hun, and aboriginal stock—all acknowledged the pontifical supremacy of the Brahmans. This paramountcy had not been gained without some concessions on the part of the priestly order to the martial element. The price the Brahmans paid to the fighters was to raise the military classes of mixed races in the social scale. In order to do so, they invented legends ascribing their birth to fire or other miraculous causes. To explore these myths is to cover interesting ground, but space forbids such excursions.

Meantime, the Aryan or Hindu religion had been undergoing great changes. The inclusion of the aboriginal population, and the Greek, Scythian, and Mongol tribes, developed the worship of snakes, devils, totems, gods, and goddesses, and accentuated the adoration of natural phenomena. The tribes with a preponderance of non-Aryan

IMPERIAL CADET CORPS.

Led by His Highness Maharaja Sir Partab Singhji.

blood found it hard to adhere strictly to the minute details of caste regulations manufactured by the Brahmans, and to conform their mode of life and habits to them. Therefore, a great variety of form, feature, civilization, and personal conduct prevailed in Hindu society, as it had been evolved by the Brahmans by the end of the 6th century.

In the beginning of the 7th century a religion was founded in the deserts of Arabia which was destined to affect profoundly the people living on the borders of Hindostan and in the Peninsula. Muhammad, born about A.D. 570, in a poor family belonging to the ruling Arab clan of Koreish, which held in its charge Abraham's temple—*Kaaba*—at Mecca, rose to denounce the idolatry and immoral practices of his contemporaneous countrymen, and their ill-treatment of women, and to preach the worship of God, one and indivisible, proclaiming himself to be the Prophet, through whom alone God could be reached. Persecution drove him out of

Mecca in 622. His flight, known as the *Hijra*, took place in 622, from which year dates the *Hijri*, or the era of Muhammad. Within eight years Muhammad had returned to Mecca, seized it, broken all the images, and made *Kaaba* the headquarters of his religion.

Within a short time of his death, which occurred two years later (632), his followers, called by the Western world Muhammadans, but styled by themselves Musalmans or professors of Islam, had established their supremacy over Arabia, Egypt, Persia, Syria, and contiguous territories, converting to their religion, at the point of the sword or by more peaceful methods, large numbers of the people they conquered. In the meantime, a propagandist of the new faith had proceeded to what is now Afghanistan, and converted the Pathans, as its inhabitants are called.

In the 8th century the Musalmans began to make incursions upon India, which, in the course of a few decades, were destined to break down the Rajput power, at that time dominant, and subject the Peninsula to successive Islamic dynasties.

The first Moslem invasion of India took place in 711, about eighty years after the death of the Prophet. It was led by Kasim, a nephew of Hejaz, an officer of the Caliph Omar, and resulted in the capture of Dwarika and of Brahmanabad, in Sind. Forty years later, however, the Rajputs rallied their force and expelled the Arabs.

The next Moslem raid was in the 10th century, when Sabuktagin, King of Ghazni, a Turk, invaded the Peninsula. After the first encounter he made a treaty with the Rajputs and retired; but returned to enforce its terms, which had not been observed.

Mahmud of Ghazni, the son of Sabuktagin, seventeen times led his forces against the Hindus, in the 11th century. Twelve of his incursions were important. He sacked many Hindu temples, destroyed the structures, melted the gold and silver idols which were enshrined in them, and carried with him plunder and slaves such as no invader had ever before obtained.

Towards the end of the 12th century, Muhammad of Ghor, leader of the Ghori Afghans, who had overthrown the dynasty of the Ghazni kings, faced the great Rajput King Prithwiraj. The first time he was defeated, and retreated. With large re-inforcements he returned to the charge and crushed the Rajputs, who, being disunited by internecine quarrels, and the surrender of their initiative to the Brahmans, were incapable of standing against determined foes.

This defeat established the Moslems upon Indian soil.

Qutab-ud-din, a slave of Muhammad Ghori, became the Emperor of India after the death of his master, founding the "Slave Dynasty," which lasted until 1288.

Jalal-ud-din then founded the Khilji dynasty, and occupied the throne of Delhi until 1321. Meanwhile, in 1303, Ala-ud-din

Khilji set forth to wipe the Rajput Rajas out of the few strongholds they had managed to retain in Rajputana. He was successful in his raid upon Chitor, and slew practically the whole garrison.

In 1321, the Tughlak dynasty overthrew the Khiljis and continued supreme till nearly the end of the 14th century.

Timur, or Tamerlane, of Tartar descent, marched his troops through India in 1398, conquering the country and laying it waste.

In the 16th century Babar invaded Hindostan, and founded the Moghul Empire, which continued until the British took over the rule of the Peninsula in 1857, deposing the last of the long line of Emperors, Bahadur Shah.

The various Moslem invasions introduced into India several new racial elements, largely of Semitic and Tartar strain; and also led to the conversion to Islam, in most cases forcibly, of millions of Hindus. Some intermixture of blood resulted between the invaders and the converts. Not a few of the

Indian Moslems claimed lineage connecting them with one or another Moslem conquering clan, although such pretensions had no foundation in fact.

It is worthy of note that the Indians who remained Hindus absolutely refused to intermingle with the Moslem conquerors. Even the lowly orders, whom Brahmanism condemned to such a debased state that the high castes looked upon their shadows as polluting and their persons as unspeakably vile, would not consent to intermarry with the followers of Muhammad. Practically the only exceptions to this rule were the representatives of a few Rajput ruling dynasties, who consented to give their daughters in marriage to the Moghul Emperors (Akbar, 1556-1605; Jahangir, 1605-1627).

The Brahmans managed to preserve the Hindu racial purity—such as it was—by their wonderful caste system, which became more and more rigid as the centuries passed by, the number of sub-castes constantly multiplying, and the rigour with which each division regulated social amenities and intermarriage with others becoming more and more accentuated. When the Moslems began to come into India, the priestly class decided to keep them out of their fold, and to this day they have remained outside the pale, even the outcast Hindus refusing to intermarry with them. It is necessary to understand this point, for it explains how Brahmanical exclusiveness has kept Hindus and Moslems in two separate camps. The two communities are divided only by religion; for racially the Hindus (217,586,892 in 1911), and Moslems (66,647,299 in the same year) are much the same, since the majority of the Indian Musalmans are descendants of Hindu converts, and comparatively few of them have a foreign strain of blood.

From what has been said it will be clear that the number of Indian Moslems who differ racially from the Hindus is comparatively small; and that the Indian professors of

Islam who have an alien strain in them form but a small percentage of the total Musalman population of India. This, however, is true of only the Peninsula proper, and is not the case with regard to those who inhabit the countries round about the north-west frontiers of India, and the territories in that region recently annexed by the British (Baluchistan and parts of the North-West Frontier Province). The population of these regions is almost entirely Musalman. The people are called Pathans, and are divided into scores of clans, including Baluchis, etc. All claim Jewish descent, and call themselves children of Israel (*Beni-Israel*). But they are mostly of Aryo-Scythian origin, and have been crossed and re-crossed by Tartar, Arab, Persian, and other blood. A large percentage of the Musalmans who serve in the Indian armies are recruited from Baluchistan, the North-West Frontier Province, and contiguous districts. Sir Herbert Risley describes them as being of Turko-Iranian stock.

Photo by courtesy of Captain Khan.

THE HON. CAPTAIN MALIK UMAR HAYAT KHAN TIWANA, C.I.E., M.V.O.

A MALIK DIN KHEL AFRIDI.

The waves of Moslem invaders who settled in Hindostan belonged to such diverse tribes that it is hard to give an idea of the heterogeneous racial elements which Islam introduced into India within the space that can be devoted to this aspect of the subject. The Arabian, Turkish, Persian, Tartar, Turanian, and Abyssinian may be mentioned as some of the strains thus introduced. These tribes, intermarrying with Indian converts of different parts of the Peninsula, have produced a great variety of peoples, each group small in numbers.

One of these races of mixed Musalmans is the Mappila or Moplah of the Madras Presidency, and the Indian States linked up with it. It is produced by the crossing of Arab with aboriginal Indian blood, with possibly a slight Indo-Aryan strain.

I deal later on in this chapter with the martial clans of Musalmans.

It is to be remembered that the arrival of

the various parties of Moslems led to considerable movements of the Hindu population. Large bodies of the military classes who were defeated took to the forests and mountains of northern India; or crossed the Vindhya Hills into the southern portion of the Peninsula. The clans that migrated mixed with the races they found in the new settlements, and not seldom brought the latter under their sway. The racial mixture which ensued ushered into existence some of the best fighters in India. For instance, the commingling of Rajput blood with the Mongoloid population of the Himalayan ranges of Nepal and contiguous country produced some of the best clans of Gurkhas.

The advent of the Europeans—the Portuguese, Dutch, French, and English—in India and their intermingling with the Indians, largely through unions not sanctioned by the church or the law, has given the Peninsula another racial combination. According to the census of 1911, the Eurasians, as they were formerly called, or Anglo-Indians[7] as they are styled now-a-days, numbered only 100,451. A considerable percentage of this community is virile. Like the Europeans in India, but unlike all except a microscopic minority of Indians, its members have the opportunity of bearing arms. They enter largely into the composition of the Volunteers, who, according to the latest available information, number somewhat under 40,000, and are regarded as an adjunct to the European Army in British India.

During the early period of European immigration an agency arose which was destined to infuse fire into the existing military classes, and even make good soldiers out of the inferior races. This was the birth of a

7. Of the two words, Eurasian (European and Asian) is more comprehensive: but since the greater percentage of the Indian Eurasians are the product of British and Indian unions, the restrictive term is not wrongly applied. However, the term Anglo-Indian has so far been used to designate Britons who, in the civil or military employ of the Government, or for trade and commerce, have made India their temporary home. Thus its newer application causes considerable complication.

new religion—Sikhism—in the Punjab. It was founded conjointly by ten Leaders, or Gurus—Nanak, 1469-1538; Angad, 1504-1552; Amar Das, 1479-1574; Ram Das, 1534-1581; Arjan, 1563-1606; Har Govind, 1595-1645; Har Rai, 1630-1661; Har Krishen, 1656-1664; Teg Bahadur, 1622-1675; and Govind Singh, 1666-1708. The years are those of birth and death, and the Gurus are named in the order in which they succeeded to Leadership.

This faith inveighed against idolatry and caste, and denied that salvation could be gained through the performance of elaborate rites. It taught that God is one; that His power is not divided with any priest or prophet; that He can be reached only by means of devotion, righteous conduct, and service to humanity; and that salvation lies in man being absorbed in the All-Good, Timeless One. The founders of this religion, especially the last five, strove to inspire their people with the determination to withstand tyranny and aggression, to take upon themselves the wrongs of the oppressed, who were too weak to revenge themselves, and to protect the defenceless.

These Teachers worked hard to give cohesion to their followers, by organizing them into a united body (later known as the *Khalsa* or pure) which should be capable of defending itself against all encroachments and of carrying on any offensive movements that might be required of it. The fundamental rules to which each member of this new society had to adhere were that he should develop his body and not merely cultivate his spirit; that he should dispel darkness from his mind, but cherish humility; that he should be ever ready to sacrifice his body, mind, and money (*tan*, *man*, *dhan*) for the sake of others; and that he should be constantly prepared to fight, without any notice, for the preservation of the community or for any other righteous cause.

The last of the long line of Gurus,

Guru Govind Singh, whose father, Guru Teg Bahadur, had been martyred by the Moghul Emperor Aurangzeb for his refusal to be converted to Islam, and for espousing the cause of persecuted Hindus, whose (Guru Govind Singh's) sons were buried alive by the Musalmans, and many of whose followers had been persecuted by the Moslem rulers, vowed that he would make one of his men fight 125,000 (*sawa lakh*) of the Moslems. He recruited into his following people of all castes and many creeds, levelled up all distinctions by means of the baptism he administered, and converted them into such good warriors that in about a century after his death the Sikhs had carved a magnificent kingdom for themselves.

This empire was lost as a result of the Sikh wars with the British, the first in 1846 and the second and last in 1849; with the exception of six States—Patiala (5,410 square miles), Jind (1,260 square miles), Nabha (930 square miles), Kapurthala (630 square miles), Faridkot (640 square miles) and Kalsia (140 square miles in area) which are ruled by Sikh Rajas in alliance with his Britannic Majesty the King-Emperor.[8] But in spite of their losses, the Sikhs gained the admiration of the British for their military genius and prowess, and ever since they have formed a large part of the Indian army and have fought valiantly for the Crown.

In speaking of the Sikhs it is always necessary to bear in mind that they are bound to one another by the tie of religion, and not of race. In some, like the Kshatriyas or Khattris, the Aryan blood predominates. In others, like the Jats, the Scythian strain is the strongest, though some deny that the Jats have any such admixture. In others, again, like the Mazbis, etc., the aboriginal element is the most pronounced.

8. Particulars about these and other States will be found in my book, *The King's Indian Allies,* to be issued by Messrs. Sampson, Low, Marston and Co., almost simultaneously with the publication of this volume. The areas given here include the territories which were granted to the Rulers of Patiala, Nabha and Jind, as a reward for the help rendered by the Rajas of those States in quelling the Indian Sepoy Mutiny in 1857.

Now that the principal influences which have evolved the fighting clans of India have been outlined, I may proceed to note down the important particulars concerning the chief amongst them:

First the principal Hindu fighting clans may be mentioned:

1. A small percentage of the Brahman caste continues to be virile. These military Brahmans are settled in the United Provinces of Agra and Oudh. They, as a rule, are tall, sturdy fellows, fair of skin, capable of the greatest endurance, especially in the matter of going without food and drink. Their capacity in the latter respect is principally due to the fact that for ages upon ages they have voluntarily subjected themselves to constant privations, cherishing, as they do, violent prejudices as to what they shall or shall not eat, and under what conditions their food shall be cooked and eaten. Not a few of these men will not partake of anything which has not been cooked by themselves. As a

rule they will not permit their wives to dine with them. Nearly all of them refuse meat. They must eat everything, even that which has been cooked by themselves, with the exception of unleavened bread fried in clarified butter (*ghee*), or the sweetmeat called *ladu*, while seated on ground that has been specially sanctified in the orthodox, Brahmanical manner. They serve exclusively in the infantry, two regiments, the 1st and 3rd Brahmans of the "Native" Army of India interlinked with each other being *entirely* composed of them.

2. The Kshatriyas, Khatris, or Chatris are the present day representatives of the old military caste of the Hindus. Only a few are to-day capable of performing military service. These men, as a rule, are fair complexioned, tall, and broad-shouldered. In the matter of eating, they are not so exclusive as the Brahmans, and most of them partake of meat whenever they can get it, and more or less indulge in intoxicating liquor.

3. The term Rajput is now restricted to a few clans of Kshatriyas which inhabit Rajputana, the Punjab, and some districts of the United Provinces of Agra and Oudh, Kathiawar, etc. Above or of medium height, broad-shouldered and stout, with regular features and a complexion the colour of wheat, pride of race is stamped on their faces and betrayed in their every gesture. They disdain all professions except ruling and bearing arms, and above all they despise agriculture. This hatred of manual occupations, coupled with their penchant for expensive marriage and other ceremonies, keeps many Rajput families poor, and not a few perennially in debt. Sad economic conditions and the strict seclusion in which their women are kept exert a degenerating effect upon their physiques, which are further undermined by the use of opium, etc. Peace also has deprived the Rajputs of that passion for keeping themselves in good form which internecine feuds or struggles with the Moghuls pro-

vided them in former times. But in spite of all these tendencies, a large portion of the Rajput population continues to furnish good fighting material. Rajputs begin to acquire skill with the sword, and learn to ride and hunt, when they are tiny tots, and in a few years become excellent horsemen, capable of galloping over the roughest country for miles together in the shortest conceivable space of time, and able to forgo food and drink for long periods. Naturally they make good cavalrymen. They also distinguish themselves in foot regiments. The sandy nature of Rajputana, necessitating the employment of camels for transport purposes, specially qualifies them to serve in camel corps, one of the most efficient of which is possessed by the Rajput Maharaja of Bikaner, Colonel his Highness Shri Sir Raj Rajeshwar Narendra Shiromani Ganga Singh Bahadur, G.C.S.I., G.C.I.E., A.D.C., Hon. LL.D. (Cambridge).

The Rajputs inhabiting the Himalayan ranges of the British Province of the Punjab and the Indian States nestling among those hills are known as Dogras. They may be designated Rajput Highlanders. Mountain life has toughened their fibre and inured them to privations, and they easily master Western drill and the use of European weapons. They chiefly serve in the infantry.

The Rajputs, including the Dogras, generally eat meat, and they are more or less addicted to opium and fond of drink. Their prejudices in regard to food are not so pronounced as those of the Brahmans, and even of the Kshatriyas, and while engaged in field service they unhesitatingly overstep the caste rules in this respect.

4. The Jats are considered to be ethnically the same as the Rajputs. In former times the two seem to have freely intermarried with each other, but now they are socially distinct. The Jats are tall, large-limbed men, of majestic and often of handsome appearance. They are capable of enduring the greatest fatigue and privation, and are among

the toughest of the military tribes. They are largely to be found in northern India, in the Punjab, Rajputana, and the United Provinces of Agra and Oudh, and generally engage in agricultural pursuits, settled in small village communities. Some of the Rajas are of Jat origin. The Jats are comparatively free from prejudices regarding eating and drinking.

5. The Gujars, Ahirs, and similar clans are racially much the same as the Jats. Their fibre, however, is not so tough. They are herdsmen by heredity, and comparatively few of them are recruited into the Army. They are well-built, hardy, sober, industrious, and thrifty.

6. The Gurkhas inhabit Nepal and adjoining districts. They are largely of Mongolian origin, but some of them have Rajput blood flowing in their veins. Their Hinduism is strongly tinctured with Buddhism, the religion which prevailed in Nepal when the Brahmans first went there, many centuries

ago, at the time of the Rajput conquest of that country. The Hindus converted the Nepalese to Brahmanism and raised the converts to the rank of Rajputs. Thus not a few of the Gurkha clans which now boast of Rajput origin have not any appreciable quantity of Rajput blood in them, but are Rajputs merely by the grace of the Brahmans. Not a few of them are the progeny of Brahmans by Nepalese women. They have very little of the Hindu prejudice respecting their food and drink. They eat meat, barring beef and the flesh of she-goats, are fond of liquors of all kinds, and use tobacco.

The Gurkhas are short—seldom above five feet five inches in height—and inclined to be stout; but the exigencies of mountain life make them hardy and quick of movement. Their sight and hearing are particularly acute. Their high cheek bones, oblique eyes, and sallow complexions betray their Mongolian origin. They serve, for the most part, in the infantry, where they have established an

Photo by courtesy of his Highness.

BODYGUARD OF HIS HIGHNESS THE MAHARAJA GAEKWAR OF BARODA.
The Maharaja is seated in the carriage.

enviable record as sure shots and daring fighters.

The national weapon is the *khukri*, or *kukri*, a knife with a broad, curved blade, about twenty inches long from the top of the handle to the point. This is carried by each Gurkha soldier in addition to his other arms, suspended from a frog attached to his waist belt. He not only plunges it into his adversary in a hand-to-hand fight, but also flings it at his foe with great force and deadly effect when the latter is out of arm's reach, seldom failing to inflict a mortal wound. It is a tradition among the Gurkhas that the *khukri* must never be drawn unless it sheds blood. They never lose a chance of practising with this weapon. With a single stroke they will cut down a tree as thick as a man's arm; and slice pieces as thin as shoe leather from the end of a branch of green wood.

The Gurkhas are famed for the night raids they make upon the enemy. They move with the stealth and noiselessness of panthers until they are right upon their unwary foes, and then they make effective use of their *khukris* and Western arms. Their wonderful sight—almost cat-like in the darkness—and their amazingly keen sense of hearing go a long way to insure their success.

The Gurkhas love manly sports of all kinds, and readily take to Western games like football. They are passionately fond of flowers, and often weave garlands of them which they wear around their necks; and keep bouquets in tumblers of water in their quarters. Many of them spend their leisure crocheting and knitting.

7. The Gharwalis resemble the Gurkhas in origin and physical characteristics. Those inhabiting the upper ranges of the Himalayas are much hardier than those who live on the lower slopes.

8. The Marathas, as a rule, have a dark complexion and irregular features. They are generally of medium height and are more

or less slender in build, though one comes across Marathas who are tall and well-proportioned. They make a speciality of rough riding across country, and are particularly adept at rapidly dashing into the enemy's domains, delivering a deadly blow, and safely retreating. They made frequent forays from their mountain fortresses in the Deccan, in the 17th Century, upon the Moghul Province of Gujerat (part of the Bombay Presidency), the Rajput States in Rajputana, and even the territories lying beyond, everywhere levying heavy contributions, much in the same manner as that in which the Germans made their exactions from the Belgians in 1914. In the course of a few decades these "mountain rats," as they were styled, gnawed away the foundations of Moslem power and established an empire of their own. Had they not come into conflict with Great Britain, they might have realized their dream of extending their sway over the whole of the Peninsula. But as the result of a series of engagements with the British, their strength was broken up, and the central Maratha power disappeared.

Large tracts of land are still under the rule of Maratha Maharajas in alliance with the King-Emperor. For instance, the Maharaja Gaekwar of Baroda, his Highness Shri Sir Sayaji Rao III., G.C.S.I., who rules a territory 8,099 square miles in extent, peopled by 2,032,798 inhabitants, is a Maratha. So also are the Maharaja of Gwalior, Honorary Major-General his Highness Sir Madho Rao Sindhia Bahadur, G.C.S.I., G.C.V.O., A.D.C., LL.D., whose State is 29,047 square miles in extent, and is populated by 3,090,798; the Maharaja of Indore, his Highness Shri Sir Tukoji Rao Holkar, G.C.S.I., whose dominions cover an area of 9,500 square miles, with 979,360 inhabitants; the Maharaja of Kolhapur, his Highness Shri Sir Shahu Chhatrapati Maharaj, G.C.S.I., G.C.I.E., G.C.V.O., LL.D., whose State, 2,855 square miles in area, is inhabited by 833,441 people; the Senior and Junior Rajas of Dewas, their Highnesses Sir Tukoji Rao, K.C.S.I., and Malhar Rao, Baba Sahib, whose combined territories are 886 square miles in area and have a population of 117,216; and the Sar Desai of Savantvadi, Shriram Savant Bhonsle Raje Bahadur, whose territories are 926 square miles in area and have a population of 217,240.[9]

Large numbers of Marathas are employed as soldiers by their own rulers, and some of them are drafted into the army maintained by British India. They serve in both the cavalry and infantry, but are especially good as troopers.

The Maratha soldiers, like the Rajputs, entertain comparatively few prejudices in regard to eating, and these they leave behind them during war times. Indeed, when they were led by men like the great Shivaji, who laid the foundation of their empire, they showed an amazing disregard of caste rules

9. For further particulars refer to my book, *The King's Indian Allies.*

and regulations, not only in the matter of eating and drinking, but even in incorporating low castes and aboriginal tribes in their confederacy. It is significant that the Maratha leaders were shrewd enough to carry the Brahmans along with them while making these innovations, by granting rewards to the priests rich enough to make it worth their while to overlook their departure from orthodoxy.

9. The military Hindus of the Carnatic or the Madras Presidency, are largely of aboriginal stock, with little, if any, Aryan intermixture. The castes which still retain their ability to bear arms generally speak Tamil, and therefore are called Tamils. Chief among them are the Kallans, Maravans, Vellalas, and Pallis. The Nayars are Malayalam speaking people, and may be described as the Kshatriyas or fighting clans of southern India, whose male members, for centuries past, occupied themselves, when peace prevailed, with various callings—agriculture,

and even washing—but in war times served as soldiers. There is very little of the Aryan strain in them. Though their appearance does not inspire confidence in their fighting capacity, yet they are hardy and capable of great endurance. They are employed largely in the regiments recruited in the Madras Presidency.

10. Lowest in the scale of Hindu fighting castes are the Paraiyans of the Madras Presidency. They are Hindu outcasts, held in such horror by their high-caste co-religionists that their very shadows are regarded as contaminating, and their touch as loathsomely polluting. They are of aboriginal stock. Their complexion is very dark, their features are irregular, and they are short and slight in build.

Each of these ten orders has numerous subdivisions, details of which have to be omitted for lack of space.

I have not included among the Hindu fighting clans a number of aboriginal martial peoples such as the Bhils, Kolis, etc. These, according to Hindu propagandists, belong to their community. Modern authorities, however, regard them as animists—worshippers of natural phenomena, spirits, etc.—and in the Census they are not incorporated with the Hindu castes and tribes. Their aboriginal descent is clear from their very dark complexion and irregular features. They are mostly found in the heart of the virgin forest, where they follow the chase and lead an open-air existence—conditions which give them great muscular strength and hardy physiques. They are held in high repute by all British officers who have had any experience with them, for, in addition to possessing courage of a very high order, they are faithful to their colours.

In regard to the Sikh fighting clans, very little needs to be added to what has been already said, because racially the different groups of Sikhs are the same as cognate Hindu castes.

The Sikh Kshatriyas are Hindu Kshatriyas whose forefathers were converted to Sikhism. It is remarkable that caste distinctions should have lingered in these people, for Sikhism is opposed to such differences, and the founders of that religion made a special effort to obliterate social invidiousness from the ranks of their followers. However, in their degenerate days caste prejudices have asserted themselves among the Sikhs. A strong effort is now being made by progressive members of the community to wipe out these differences; but since they exist at present, it would be wrong to ignore them in this book.

The Sikh Jats are ethnically the same as the Hindu Jats. Doubtless the martial religion of the Sikhs has helped to toughen the already hardy fibre of this race. It may be added that a very large proportion of the total Sikh population consists of Jats.

In regard to the other Sikh clans which furnish recruits for the Armies in India, that of the Mazbis has been mentioned. The Mazbis have very little Aryan stock in them, and are regarded as the remnants of the aborigines of northern India. Some of their confrères are engaged in such occupations as scavenging, the work most abhorred by the Hindus. Their features are irregular and they are not tall and stalwart, as are the Sikh Jats—but their ability to bear inclement weather, fatigue, and privation is practically limitless. They specially excel as sappers and miners, and largely fill the Pioneer regiments of the British Indian Infantry. The effect of Sikhism on the mettle of this class is most pronounced. Truly, that faith has made manly men out of cowards.

Similar in social status, physique, and fighting qualities to the Mazbis are the Ramdasias, who also are employed in Pioneer regiments.

Speaking of the Sikhs as a whole, it may be said that each class is subdivided into petty groups. However, caste prejudices are not so strong among them as they are in the high class Hindus. In one point, however, they are very strict—they do not use tobacco in any shape or form.

The Sikh is noted for his brilliant bayonet charge. He holds the butt of his gun with both hands, and mercilessly drives the steel into the abdomen or ribs of his foe.

Now to refer to the Moslem fighting clans of India:

Many of them are racially the same as the Hindus.

The Moslem Jats are the descendants of Hindu Jats, who went over to Islam.

The Moslem Rajputs are Hindu Rajputs whose forefathers embraced the faith promulgated by the Prophet Muhammad.

The Moslem Gujars and Ahirs are akin to the Hindu tribes of the same name.

The Hindustani Musalmans, as they are termed by the British-Indian military authorities, are Moslems of the United Provinces of Agra and Oudh, and contiguous districts.

They are either the progeny of Hindu converts of Islam who were Aryo-Scythians, or are the descendants, more or less pure, of the original Moslem peoples who conquered India in the centuries long past.

Similarly the term Punjabi Musalman is used to describe the descendants of Hindu converts to the faith of Muhammad domiciled in the Punjab. These men are ethnically Aryo-Scythians. Not a few of them are Jats, Gujars, Ahirs, Tiwanas, etc. Nothing further needs to be said about these Moslem tribes.

I have also referred to the Mappilas, a mixture of Arab and aboriginal stock. They, like their compatriots, the Hindus of the Madras Presidency, are not majestic in appearance, but they bear privation and fatigue without complaint, and their spirit is not to be daunted by any difficulties that may be placed in their path as soldiers of the King-Emperor.

There still remain to be mentioned the

Moslem fighters, inhabiting the north-western corner of India and neighbouring territories, who profess to be of Semitic descent, though very few of them can really substantiate this claim. As has been shown, they are really Aryo-Scythian, with some Turkish, Tartar, Persian, Turanian, and Mongolian admixture; though a few (the Afghans and Baluchis) really have more or less Jewish blood in them.

Those inhabiting Afghanistan and the contiguous mountain districts, and their descendants who have migrated to various parts of India, are generically known as Pathans. The cold climate and the hardy life of the mountains of Afghanistan and north-western India have preserved their virility. Broadly speaking, they are tall, stalwart, handsome fellows, usually with regular features and fair complexion, some of them with blue or grey eyes.

The Pathan tribes of Indian or Pactyan stock are the Waziris, Bannuchis, Dawris,

Tane, Khattak, Afridi, Utman Khel, Jadran, Bangash, Orakzai, Dilazak, Hanni, Wardag, Mangal, and Bitanni. Those of Afghan descent are the Muhammadzai, Shinwari, Yusafzai, Tarklanri, Surgiani, Mullagori (more likely of Indian stock), Mohmund, Daudzai, Khalil, Chamkani or Chakmani, and Zirani. Those of Scythian stock are the Kakar, Ushtarani, Bakhtiar and Shirani. The tribes of pure Afghan stock are the Abdalli or Duranni, Tarin, Miana, and Baraich. Those of mixed Turkish and Afghan stock are the Khugianni; and the Ghilzai tribes consisting of the Hotak, Kharoti, Tokhi, and Nasar clans, known as the Turan Pathans; the Suleman Khel, Ali Khel, Akha Khel, Ishaq, Andar and Tarakki, known as the Ibrahimzais; and the Lodi tribes, the Dutanni, Naizi or Niazai, Sur, Prangi, Sarwani, Khasor, Marwat, Mian Khel, Daulat Khel and Tator, known as the Lohani Pathans.

A number of the Moslem clans inhabiting Baluchistan are known as Baluchis, all claiming Semitic descent and even professing to be descended from the Arab stock of their Prophet Muhammad. Their pretensions in regard to kinship with the founder of their religion are not established, but many of them undoubtedly have Arab blood in their veins. They are so similar to the Pathans in their racial characteristics that it is not necessary, in view of the limited space at my disposal, to describe them further. A marked trait of character of the Baluchi is his desire to fight on even terms with his foe—to engage in a hand-to-hand combat with shield and sword rather than to fire at the enemy from a distance. He learns to be a good marksman and is very much prized by British officers for his fidelity and tractability.

The chief tribes of the Baluchis are the Rind, Laghari, Jatoi, Gurchani, Lashari, Khosa, Korai, Tibbi-Lund, Chandia, Gopang, Mazari, Hot, Nutkani, Gurmani, Kulachi, Quasrani, Jiskani, Drishak, Marri, Petafi, Gashkori, Mihrani, Bozdar, Mastoi,

Mashori, Dasti, Hajani, Shahrani, Sanjrani, Laskani, Magassi, Ahmadani, Gabol, Quandrani, Kupchani, Aliani, Kashak, Khetran, Bugti or Bogti, Bujrani, Badai, Pachar, Tanwari, Jafar, Hijbani, Sargani, Shekhani, Shahani, Lund, Mariani, Sakhani, and Mazkani.

Lastly I may note a few facts concerning the Christian fighting clans of India, mostly belonging to the Madras Presidency. They are largely of Dravidian stock, with some Semitic blood in them, introduced by the Syrians who settled in southern India in the early centuries of the Christian era, the pioneer among them reputed to have been St. Thomas, the doubting apostle of Christ. The members of this community have, for centuries, possessed warlike instincts, and their soldierly spirit continues to this day, making them eminently fitted to fight the battles of the Empire.

There is no space to describe how these diverse clans live in their settlements, nor

Photo by G. T. Jones & Son, Kingston-on-Thames.

A Group of Officers and Men of the 15th Ludhiana Sikhs.
(Note the quoits on the turbans).

whom, what, and how they worship; but a few words may be said concerning the outward appearance of the chief among them.

The Sikh soldier is easily distinguished by the voluminous turban he winds about his head. He does not trim his beard, which he twists up in a roll and ties over his ears, and which, when uncurled and left to hang as nature intended it to do, falls over his breast. When he takes off his turban it is discovered that his hair has never been cut, and his long locks are coiled in a knot on top of his head, held in place by a small comb which his religion bids him wear. He is usually a tall, broad-shouldered man and takes gigantic strides when he walks.

The Sikh sometimes wears a quoit—a steel disc, six to eight inches in diameter, and about one-half or three-fourths of an inch wide, with a razor-sharp edge—around his turban; and employs it as a deadly weapon. He flings it with great force at the enemy from a distance, and seldom fails to cut off his head.

The Gurkha may be singled out in a crowd on account of his short, squat form and his Mongolian cast of countenance. He wears a small, black, round, visorless cap at a rakish angle.

The Pathan winds his turban, usually of shorter length than that used by the Sikh, around a conical cap (*kullah*). He often lets the end of his turban hang down over his shoulder. His black locks show under the edge of his head-dress, and his beard and moustache are trimmed.

Many of the Musalman soldiers have no beard, but shave their faces clean except for a moustache, which is kept trimmed short, as their religion forbids them to allow their moustaches to grow long enough for the hairs to touch the lips.

Many Rajput soldiers part their beards in the middle and brush them straight back in a fashion that gives them a fierce look.

CHAPTER III.

The Indian Armies.

THE fittest from among the fighting clans, about 580,000 in all, are borne on the rosters of Indian armies of various descriptions—standing, mounted police, military police, militia, levies, and reserves.

Some of these troops are employed by the Government of British India. Some are maintained by the various Rajas. The number is about evenly divided between the two sets of administrators.

To deal first with the Indians in British Indian Armies, etc.:

Of the Indian soldiers serving in British India, the largest number is employed in the "Native" Army. According to the last *Statistical Abstract relating to British India,* covering the period from 1902-3 to 1911-12, it possessed, exclusive of "native" artificers and followers, 159,861 Indian officers and men, 2,772 British officers, and 341 British Warrant and Non-Commissioned Officers, or 162,974 in all. It consisted of five sections:

Officers, N.C.O.s, and Men:

Artillery	10,043
Body-Guards ...	422
Cavalry	24,250
Sappers and Miners.	5,154
Infantry	119,992
Total ...	159,861[1]

Particulars regarding the strength and composition of various branches of the "Native" Army will be given later.

About 35,000[2] Indian soldiers were employed in 1912-13 on the British Indian auxiliary forces. These were in addition to 37,382

1. P. 219.

2. *Statement exhibiting the Moral and Material Progress and Condition of India during the year 1911-12, and the nine preceding years*, p. 329.

volunteers, all efficients, practically all Europeans and semi-Europeans. The Military Police had a total strength of about 21,500. Those serving in the Border Military Police, Militia, and Levies numbered altogether about 13,500. These are generally included in the military strength possessed by India. They are capable of performing light cavalry duty, and are used to maintain peace in the unsettled districts of Burma, the North-West Frontier Province, Baluchistan, etc. They are usually armed with Martini-Henry or Snider rifles and carbines, but are not under military authority, being controlled by civil and political agencies. Space forbids further allusion to them.

The actual strength of the "Native" Army Reserve List on 1st April, 1913, was 33,712.[3] It is intended to raise the sanctioned strength of this body to 50,000. I advert to this subject further on in this chapter.

3. *Ibid.*, *1912-13*, p. 127.

To sum up, in round figures, the strength of the "Native" Army, Auxiliary Forces (excluding Volunteers), and Reserves exceeds, at present, 231,000. The "Native" Army, possessing about 163,000 officers and men, alone deserves to be considered at length, and is referred to in its proper place later on.

Here I may interject that quite apart from its Indian soldiery, the British Government of India maintains an "European" Army. It consists of detachments from the Army employed in the United Kingdom, placed by the British War Office at the disposal of the British Indian Government, and paid for by the latter Administration so long as it is thus detailed. According to the latest available figures, it has an established strength of 75,573 officers and men, all Britons, not including artificers and followers, all Indian.[4] It consists of:

4. *Statistical Abstract Relating to British India from 1902-3 to 1911-12*, p. 219.

Officers, N.C.O.s, and Men:

Royal Artillery ...	15,769
Cavalry	5,634
Royal Engineers ...	307
Infantry	53,746
Officers, attached, etc.	117
	75,573

Adding the European to the Indian Force, the total is over 306,000 (or 343,000 if Volunteers are included); or 238,000 if only the "Native" and European Armies are taken into consideration, and Auxiliary Troops of all descriptions and Reservists are excluded.

This book is not directly concerned with the European branch of the Indian Army. All that it is necessary to add is that the "European" and "Native" Armies (238,000) are brigaded together, forming a unified system, under the orders of the Commander-in-Chief in India.

The conjoint force is divided into two

Commands, one known as the Northern and the other as the Southern Army.

The first, commanded by Lieutenant-General Sir J. Willcocks, K.C.B., K.C.S.I., K.C.M.G., D.S.O., has its headquarters at Murree. It comprises five Divisions, namely, the 1st (Peshawar), 2nd (Rawal Pindi), 3rd (Lahore), 7th (Meerut), and 8th (Lucknow) Divisions. The name of each indicates its headquarters. Besides these five divisions there are three frontier brigades.

The headquarters of the Southern Army, with General Sir J. E. Nixon, K.C.B., the General Officer Commanding, is at Ootacamund, in the Madras Presidency. It consists of the 4th (Quetta), 5th (Mhow), 6th (Poona), 9th (Secunderabad), and the Burma Divisions, their headquarters being Quetta, Mhow, Poona, Ootacamund, and Maymyo respectively. Besides these Divisions there is a garrison at Aden, which forms a part of British India.

Each Division consists roughly of 20,000

officers and men, the proportion of Indians and British being rather more than two to one. It comprises Cavalry, Artillery, Sappers and Miners, Infantry, Supply and Transport equipment, etc., and is a self-sufficing unit.

Affairs are so managed that in spite of the fact that the Indians are more than twice the British in actual strength, the number of British artillerymen greatly preponderates in each Division. This procedure is a legacy of the Sepoy Mutiny. Before that political convulsion, the number of Indians serving in the Artillery (*golandaz*, as they were called) was very large. Since then, however, not only has the number been cut down, but Indian artillerymen are employed in minor positions, and have practically no place in the heavy batteries. Most of the Indian artillerymen are in the Mountain Batteries, which are a special feature of the Indian military organization, the exigencies of fighting in the mountainous regions of Northern India, especially the

North-West Frontier, having led to this development. Some Indians are employed in the European corps of Artillery. They have not been included in the figures given for the European Artillery, but have been incorporated with those serving in the purely Indian Artillery. It needs to be clearly pointed out that the ranks of the Indian artillerymen are so shrewdly divided up by the introduction of European gunners that the power of the former to cause serious trouble is minimized most effectively.

To the detachments of the corps of Royal Engineers incorporated in a Division falls the same work (clearing forests and débris, making roads, building bridges, etc.) that is performed by the Sappers and Miners in the Indian Army. The Royal Engineers being a numerical minority, initiate and supervise measures which are carried out by the Indian Sappers and Miners. In times of peace they concern themselves with erecting and repairing Defence Works.

The policy of giving inferior weapons to Indians was abandoned some time ago, and during recent years much effort has been made to bring the armament of the Indian Cavalry and Infantry up to the standard demanded by modern requirements. The crack Indian Cavalry have now Lee-Enfield rifles, some, in addition, bearing lances, and being therefore called Lancers, while others have swords. The best Infantry battalions bear Lee-Metford rifles. When the scheme of re-arming the Indian soldiers, now being rapidly pushed forward, has been carried into effect, all of them will be thus equipped.

The Indian soldiers wear the European uniform—serges for winter and parade, and khaki for summer manœuvres and field service.[5] The colour of the serge varies with

5. It is interesting to note that the world owes the work *khaki* to India. Imported into the Peninsula by Musalmans, it means "made of earth," or "the colour of earth." It is now current in all languages spoken by civilized and semi-civilized peoples. The dust-colour has been found eminently suited for manœuvres and active service; and khaki uniform is now prescribed by most nations for these purposes.

the different regiments and services. Thus the Infantry wear tunics of blue, red, drab, or dark blue, knickerbockers, gaiters or *puttees*, and ankle boots. Sappers are dressed in red, and artillerymen in blue. All uniforms have bright facings. The Indians, as a rule, are not given European headgear, but, as noted in the preceding chapter, either wear turbans tied in a variety of ways, or caps. The brilliant colours of the uniforms, with flashes here and there of gold or silver lace, and the rainbow hues of the turbans, make a parade of Indian soldiers a sight never to be forgotten, profoundly impressing the pomp-loving Easterner and the pageant-worshipping Westerner alike.

The Indian soldier is drilled with great patience in European tactics of warfare, usually by an Indian who has thoroughly mastered the Western mode of drilling, and is particularly good at explaining it to others. The superior officers in every Indian regiment, including the Commandant and the Commanders of each of the four squadrons or double companies into which each regiment is divided, are all Britons. They usually receive their training in Great Britain, though recently a staff college has been established at Quetta. When attached to the Indian list, a British officer serves for a year in a European regiment before he passes on to the "Native" Army.

The highest rank which an Indian can hold is that of Commander of a company, or half-squadron. The senior among these Company Commanders is known as *Risaldar* Major in the Cavalry, and *Subadar* Major in the Infantry, and he assists the Commandant in managing the regiment. The other seven Company Commanders are called *Risaldars* or *Ressaidars* in the Cavalry, and *Subadars* in the Infantry.

Since 1901 provision has been made for Indians of royal and noble blood to be trained in the Imperial Cadet Corps, organized by Lord Curzon, Viceroy and Governor-General of India from 1899 to 1905. On the completion of their three years' course they are given commissions as Subalterns, and are placed upon the "Native Indian Land Forces" list, from which officers may be attached to Indian, but not European regiments. However, at present, only eleven are borne on this register, eight with the rank of Lieutenant, and three with that of 2nd Lieutenant.

A few Indians have been honoured for their conspicuous gallantry, or their distinguished position in life, with honorary ranks ranging from Lieutenant to Major-General. Some of the men have been attached as *Aides-de-Camp*, honorary or otherwise, to his Majesty the King-Emperor, their Excellencies the Viceroy and Governor-General, the Commander-in-Chief in India, etc., while others have been attached to one or another regiment, or merely given the rank, if they are on the retired list.

The exclusion of Indians from the higher

ranks is a vexed question. Indian military men naturally wish to rise higher than *Risaldar* Major and *Subadar* Major, and Indian civilians sympathize with their ambition. A very strong case can be made out to support the Indian aspirations. A single fact that may be mentioned is that Indians have shown themselves to be excellent leaders of fighters from time immemorial; and that not many decades ago they marshalled their forces so cleverly against their Western foes that they extorted the admiration and praise of a number of European authorities. However, the powers that be seem to consider that Indians are good only as soldiers of the line and petty officers, but need to be led by Westerners. These dicta are attributed by some to that disposition which monopoly breeds among men. It is not the design of this book to enter into controversies: I content myself with merely stating the pros and cons in as impartial a manner as I can employ.

Leaving such considerations aside, it is

admitted by all who can speak with authority on the subject that India's fighters can and do make effective use of Western weapons and Occidental tactics of warfare. The Divisional unit of the Indian Army, therefore, composed though it is of men with brown and with white skins, is yet, from the point of view of military efficiency, a homogeneous body. Climatic influences have given different complexions to the British and Indian soldiers, but beneath the different colours, the same blood courses in their veins, the racial antecedents of the two being very much the same.

And to both of them is given the privilege of fighting under the same flag, and the task of conserving the interests of the same Empire. For over a century British and Indian soldiers have fought side by side under many skies, and many conditions.

I fervently hope, if in the future, warfare should retard the march of human civilisation, they will be found standing shoulder to shoulder against any common foes that may confront them, as they were doing on the Continent of Europe in the closing months of 1914.

The present organization of the European and "Native" Armies has been brought about by a series of reforms which extended over many decades, and were given their final shape by Lord Kitchener during his term of office as Commander-in-Chief in India, extending from 1902 to 1909. To Lord Kitchener belongs the credit of abolishing the old system which split up the forces into five commands. He divided the troops into two commands, and concentrated the bulk of the soldiery near and on the North-West Frontier, ready for use in any emergency. He also worked strenuously to improve the standing army to a level at which it would be capable of being almost instantaneously mobilized, and would ever be in prime fighting condition. He improved the existing arrangements for supplying officers to serve in regiments, and in the divisional and other commands and at Army headquarters; for breeding and importing mounts and remounts for the Cavalry; and for manufacturing and purchasing arms and equipment for all branches of the Army. The reorganization of the Supply and Transport Corps, and of the Ordnance Department, the improvement of the Indian Medical Service, and the new methods of preparing and submitting military accounts and correspondence that were introduced, were no less important reforms which were carried out by Lord Kitchener.

His successor, General Sir O'Moore Creagh, G.C.B., G.C.S.I., Commander-in-Chief till 8th March, 1914, advanced these and other Army reforms, and Sir Beauchamp Duff, who took over the command on that date, wisely followed in the footsteps of his predecessors.

The result is that the Armies of British India, both Indian and European, are now capably officered and drilled, and are able to use the various weapons provided them with deadly effect on the enemy. The mounts and arms of the Cavalry, and the equipment of the Infantry and other branches of the military service leave nothing to be desired. Arrangements for the supply of food and fodder, and the transport of men and animals and their belongings, and the agency responsible for the care of the troops in the regimental line and on active service, have been carried to a point of perfection well worthy of emulation by other countries. Military efficiency in modern times requires constant attention and incessant progress in all directions, and these duties are conscientiously and capably carried out by the Commander-in-Chief.

Now that the general plan of the military organization of the Indian Army has been set down, I may proceed with the description of the composition and character of the "Native" Army in British India.

Certain broad facts common to the Indian soldiers employed in the various branches of the Army—Cavalry, Infantry, Artillery, Sappers and Miners, etc.—may first be outlined.

The Indian is not impressed into the Army by a conscript system, but elects, of his own free will, to join the colours. The only possible exception that could be mentioned is that tribes on the North-West Frontier, in accordance with time-honoured custom, are required to furnish "levies," which are employed to keep the turbulent clansmen in order. These forces serve on outposts in tribal areas, from which Lord Curzon withdrew regular troops.

Men between the ages of sixteen and twenty-five may enlist. The height and measurements vary for different services, and will be referred to when I treat separately of the Cavalry, Infantry, etc.

Technically speaking, an Indian joins a regiment for three years, at the end of which period he may obtain his discharge unless war is raging at the time, when the term is automatically extended to the close of active operations. But all this is mere red tape. Once allowed to enter the army, the Indian, as a rule, stays there as long as he may—until he is invalided or pensioned.

Generally speaking, the recruits come from the land-owning and farming classes. Men from the same family or tribe, and from the same locality, find their way into the same regiment, or those linked up together. The work of the recruiting officers is often made easy by the advertising voluntarily done by those already following the colours.

To take advantage of the strongly marked gregarious instinct of the Indian peoples, and to give full scope to it, the regiments are formed on the principle of "class-companies," that is to say, the men in a company all profess the same religion, frequently come from the same district, and are related to one another, or belong to the same caste, and all have common fighting traditions. The various bonds of union conduce to *esprit de corps* in the company, and by reducing the prejudices in the matter of food, etc., to one common level, make its management easier.

In some cases the entire regiment is composed of a single class of men. This is especially true of the Gurkha, Brahman, and some Sikh regiments. The advantages of such an organization are counterbalanced by the fact that in case of mutiny this kind of a regiment would be far more dangerous than one with mixed nationalities. For this reason there is a strong disposition on the part of the military authorities to make the company, but not the regiment, homogeneous. In fact, the present policy seems to be to combine in one regiment companies of different peoples more or less antagonistic to each other. For instance, a regiment may be composed of four companies of Sikhs and four of Musalmans; or of two companies of Sikhs, two of Dogras, two of Punjabi Musalmans, and two of Hindustani Musalmans. In some cases, even a greater mixture of races is effected.

This idea of promoting *esprit de corps*

through uniformity as regards class and clan has been carried to the extent of linking up with each other regiments of the same composition. The 1st and 3rd Brahmans, for instance, consisting, as their name signifies, of Brahmans, may be cited as instances of linked battalions. These have the same regimental centre.

The system has been so elaborated that a soldier who enlists in one of the regiments may be required to serve in another linked up with it. This is done in order to maintain the strength and efficiency of the battalions in the field. Under the "linked" system the supply of trained men can be constantly kept up to the proper standard, instead of depending for reinforcements upon recruits, or volunteers from other corps, as was the case under the old plan.

The Indian soldier is, as a rule, a married man, and he brings his relations to live in the regimental line, where each family is given separate quarters, generally consisting of a small mud hut, with proper provision for the seclusion (*purdah*) of women. Each forms part of a large block of houses of similar description, set as close together, side by side, as they can be built.

Children are born and grow up in the line, and some of the sons join their father's regiment. The military authorities, however, prefer recruits from the outside, to many of these "line-boys." Certain classes of the latter are in demand, and are given allowances regulated according to a definite scale.

So attached is the Indian soldier to his near, and even distant, relations, that his superior officers have to see to it that he does not bring too many of them to live with him to "eat up" all his pay.

Apart from all other considerations, any laxity in this regulation would have a deteriorating effect upon the physique of the Indian fighter: for he does not feed at Government expense, and is likely to stint himself to support his kinsmen.

Living as he generally does with his family, the food is prepared by the wife or some other woman relative. But so strict are some soldiers, chiefly Brahmans, that they insist upon cooking their own victuals. Some of the unmarried fighters make a private arrangement among themselves whereby each helps in the cooking of the meals, which they eat together. A few cooks are usually allotted to a regiment. They prepare meals for those who do not scruple to eat food cooked by others, and prefer not to take the trouble to prepare it themselves.

Each regiment has its own bazaar (market place), where provisions of all kinds, haberdashery, etc., can be purchased. The shopkeepers are selected by the authorities, who exercise more or less rigorous control over them.

The Indian soldier—officer and private alike—is required to buy his own victuals. Since prices in India fluctuate considerably, it is deemed advisable to deduct 4s. 8d. (Rs. 3/8) monthly from his pay, in lieu of which the regimental shopkeepers (the *banias*) are authorized to issue rations to him according to a scale laid down by the authorities.

This system is intended to save the soldier worry about famine prices. It does this effectively, so far as he is concerned. But in spite of this provision he has to buy food for his dependents at current rates. I may parenthetically add that Indians in the Army have to pay for their uniforms, etc.

The shopkeepers also furnish supplies to the relatives left behind by the soldiers proceeding on active service, though it may be noted that when the Indian fighter goes to the front, his relatives usually move back to their villages to live among their kinsfolk.

Here I may add that each regiment has priests, usually one of each creed represented in it, who minister to the men of their faith. These religious teachers serve to keep the fighting tradition associated with such warlike religions as Sikhism and Islam ever before their flock. They also keep up the moral tone of the officers and men. Their influence is exerted against intemperance and, in passing, it may be noted that the temperance movement has made great headway in the Indian Army during recent years. The priests promote literacy among the soldiers, which purpose is likewise advanced by the teachers provided by Government for each regiment. Some recruits actually profess to join the Army for the sake of learning to read, write, and keep accounts.

Besides the priests, teachers, and cooks, there are numerous other followers attached to each regiment, who perform such functions as pitching tents, carrying water, looking after conservancy, repairing shoes, attending to the horses, etc.

The Indian soldiers in the regimental lines celebrate with great enthusiasm the religious and semi-religious festivals that mark their calendars. Hymns, to the accompaniment of instruments of all sorts, some of which give out sounds that are weird to the

Western ear, are sung in the temples within the lines. Some, the Gurkhas, for instance, offer animal sacrifices at the altar of their gods and goddesses. To give an example, during the Dusehera festival, which is celebrated in honour of the goddess *Kali* and lasts ten days, the Gurkhas pile their arms, erect tents for the accommodation of the spectators who have been invited, and with great dexterity sever the heads of the buffaloes that are sacrificed. The children act as sacrificial agents in the case of goats.

In this connection it will be of interest to note that the various clans employed in the Army have their distinctive war cries, which lend a dramatic interest to the campaigns in which they are engaged side by side with less emotional troops. The Sikh, for instance, shouts at the top of his voice: "*Shri-Wah-i-Guru-ji-ka-Khalsa!*" ("Victory by the grace of God," or "Victory unto God"); and "*Sat-Sri-Akal!*" ("True is the Timeless One"). The Musalman yells "*Allah-o-Akbar!*"

("God is great"). Many of the Hindu soldiers cry, "*Jai Kali!*" or "*Jai Ram!*" ("Victory by the grace of the Goddess"—or "Victory by God's Grace").

The superior Indian officers in the "Native" Army are said to hold commissions. These "commissions," however, are not the same as those granted to the British officers serving in this or in other armies, but are of inferior grade, if not technically, at least so in actual fact, for they do not entitle those who hold them to advance higher than *Risaldar* Major or *Subadar* Major. These remarks do not apply to the few who have graduated from the Imperial Cadet Corps, and have been placed on the "Native Indian Land Forces" list.

Only twenty-five per cent. of the posts held by Indian Commissioned Officers are reserved for men who receive direct commissions. These are bestowed upon young men belonging to leading families which have distinguished themselves in serving the

Government. These men must needs satisfy the military requirements in respect of age, physique, intelligence, education, etc. They serve as *Jemadars* (Indian Lieutenants) for a year on probation, before they are confirmed.

The other seventy-five per cent. of the commissioned posts which Indians can hold are given to the men who have risen from the ranks, or to Non-Commissioned Officers, for distinguished service. Until some time ago these men were given all, and not merely three-fourths of such appointments, as the system of direct commissions did not then exist.

Having described the general conditions of the "Native" Army, I may now relate the important particulars concerning some of the principal branches of military service.

Most of the Cavalry regiments are composed of officers and men to whom mounts, remounts, and equipment, with the exception of rifles, are not supplied by the Government at its own expense. They must, therefore, make themselves responsible for purchasing these requisites in the first instance, and for renewing them as needed, or as required by the regulations. The trooper, on joining, agrees that a portion of his pay shall be deducted monthly, and credited to the regimental fund, from which are purchased the mounts, equipment, uniforms, etc. In the same way, the cavalrymen provide the forage for their horses. This is known as the *Silladar* system, and is a modification of one which has prevailed in India for centuries.

The Cavalry regiments which are not organized on this basis are termed *non-Silladar*. In such a case the authorities have to make themselves responsible for mounting the trooper, arming and equipping him, feeding his horse, and furnishing remounts if they are required.

Comparatively few regiments of the Indian Cavalry, however, consist of out-and-out mercenaries. As a general rule, Indians of the better class, petty land-owners, well-to-do farmers, etc., join the ranks of the troopers, and they elect to serve on the *Silladar* basis.

Enlistment in both classes of Cavalry is entirely voluntary. Candidates must be between sixteen and twenty-five years of age. The Officer Commanding a Cavalry Regiment may accept a recruit at his discretion, irrespective of his height.

A Cavalry regiment, as a rule, consists of 640 officers and men.

Thirty-two of the officers hold commissions. Of these, fifteen of the superior ranks are practically always held by British. The seventeen inferior ones are always held by Indians.

Each regiment is subdivided into four squadrons consisting of 160 officers and men.

Each squadron is subdivided into a company of eighty units.

At the head of the regiment is the Commandant, invariably a British Officer, usually with the rank of Lieutenant-Colonel.

Each squadron is placed under a

Squadron Commander, always a British officer, the senior among the Squadron Commanders being Second-in-Command of the regiment, and usually holding the rank of Lieutenant-Colonel.

The Squadron Commanders are assisted by Squadron Officers, nine in number, all of them British, and ranging from Major to Second Lieutenant in rank. In very isolated instances Indian graduates from the Imperial Cadet Corps have been attached to Indian regiments to qualify themselves to hold the rank of Squadron Commander.

There also is a Medical Officer, sometimes two. He is a physician and surgeon, who has successfully passed the test for the Indian Medical Service, for which examinations are annually held in London, and who has received his commission. He holds rank in the Army, and advances by regular stages. A few Indians have voyaged to the British Isles, and have succeeded, in competition with Britons, in entering this Service. Many of these men, however, have been given civil appointments in different parts of the Peninsula, a few alone being attached to regiments as Medical Officers.

Among the Indian officers, the senior is *Risaldar* Major. Technicalities aside, he is the Indian Commandant of the regiment, and all orders pass through him from the British Officer commanding the regiment to the troops. In addition to such duties, he commands a company, or half-squadron. The *Risaldar* Major—distinguished by a crown on each shoulder strap—receives a consolidated pay of £20 (Rs. 300)[6] per mensem, if he is a *Silladar*, or £10 (Rs. 150), plus £3 6s. 8d. allowance for acting as senior Indian officer in his regiment if he is a *non-Silladar*.

The remaining seven companies are headed by *Risaldars* or *Ressaidars*. Of the

6. All figures pertaining to salaries, allowances, etc., of officers and men that are given in this chapter are taken from the latest available issue of *Army Regulations, India*, prepared by the Government of India. R.1/-/- = 1s. 4d.

Pays and allowances in all cases are for the month, unless expressly stated otherwise.

The salaries vary a little in some regiments.

former there generally are three, and of the latter four. The *Risaldar* receives a consolidated pay of £16 13s. 4d. (Rs. 250) if he is a *Silladar*, or £10 (Rs. 150) if he is a *non-Silladar*. The *Ressaidar* is given £10 (Rs. 150) if he is a *Silladar*, or £7 6s. 8d.(Rs. 110) if he is a *non-Silladar*. The *Risaldar* wears three and the *Ressaidar* two stars on his shoulder straps. These officers may be likened respectively to Majors and Captains in the British Army.

Each Cavalry company has its own *Jemadar* (Indian Lieutenant). Generally, one of them acts as Indian Adjutant, and is known as *Woordie* Major; though sometimes a regiment is given an additional *Jemadar* to act in this capacity. The *Jemadar* has a single star on his shoulder straps. His pay is £5 6s. 8d. (Rs. 80), if he is a *Silladar*, and £4 (Rs. 60) if he is a *non-Silladar*. If he is a *Woordie* Major he is given, in addition, £2 13s. 4d. (Rs. 40) if a *Silladar*, or £1 3s. 4d. (Rs. 17/8/-) if not.

All *non-Silladar* officers receive an allowance (*batta*), ranging between £3 6s. 8d. (Rs. 50) and 10s. 8d. (Rs. 8) per month so long as they are on field or foreign (including Colonial) service.

Officers who, for conspicuous bravery, have been admitted into the "Order of British India" receive 2s. 8d. (Rs. 2) *per diem* if they hold one of the 188 first-class appointments, each of which carries the title of *Sardar* (Chief), prefixed to the name, and *Bahadur* (Brave), affixed to the same name. An officer receives only 1s. 4d. (R. 1) a day if he holds one of the 250 second-class appointments, which carries only the title of *Bahadur*.

Officers may hold the "Indian Order of Merit" irrespective of the "Order of British India." This is of three classes, first, second, and third, each carrying its own scale of allowance graded according to the rank of the recipient. The Indian Order of Merit is bestowed upon those who distinguish themselves in the firing line, and, as will be shown

Photos by G. T. Jones & Son, Kingston-on-Thames.

SIKH INFANTRY OFFICERS.

Sardar RAM SINGH *Bahadur.* BALWANT SINGH *Bahadur.*

later, is not confined merely to commissioned officers.

The non-commissioned ranks immediately below the *Jemadar* are:

The Farrier Major, who receives £3 (Rs. 45) if a *Silladar*, or £1 12s. 0d. (Rs. 24) if he is a *non-Silladar*.

The *Daffadar*, corresponding to Sergeant, who has the same pay as the Farrier Major. If he acts as *Kot Daffadar* Major (Quarter-master-Sergeant), Drill *Daffadar* (Drill Sergeant), Orderly *Daffadar* (Orderly Sergeant), Trumpet Major, etc., he gets "extra-duty pay" in addition to the appointment which he holds.

The Farrier *Daffadar*, employed only in the *non-Silladar* Cavalry, who receives £1 12s. 0d. (Rs. 24).

The Lance *Daffadar*, who is paid £2 13s. 4d. (Rs. 40) if a *Silladar*, and £1 6s. 8d. (Rs. 20) if a *non-Silladar*.

The *Salutri*, or veterinary assistant, who is paid £3 12s. 0d. (Rs. 54) a month.

The Trumpeter, who receives £2 14s. 8d. (Rs. 41) if a *Silladar*, and £1 6s. 8d. (Rs. 20) if he is a *non-Silladar*.

The Farrier Pupil in the *non-Silladar* Cavalry regiment, who receives £1 1s. 4d. (Rs. 16).

The *Sowar*, or Trooper, mounted on horseback or on a camel, who receives £2 5s. 4d. (Rs. 34), if he furnishes and feeds his own animal, and 17s. 4d. (Rs. 13) if he is a *non-Silladar*. The *Silladar Sowar* is given an extra allowance if the price of forage rises above a certain stipulated figure.

A Farrier, who receives the same pay as a *Sowar*, if he is in the *Silladar* Cavalry, or £1 7s. 6⅓d. (Rs. 20/10/4) if he is a *non-Silladar*.

The Ward Orderly, who is paid £1 1s. 10d. (Rs. 16/6/-) if a *Silladar*, and 17s. 4d. (Rs. 13) if a *non-Silladar*.

The Assistant *Salutri*, who receives £2 5s. 4d. (Rs. 34), in the *Silladar* Cavalry.

The Recruit in the *Silladar* Cavalry, who

is paid £1 1s. 10d. (Rs. 16/6/-) or, in some instances, only 18s. 8d. (Rs. 14/-/-).

Every two *Sowars* have a groom (*syce*) between them, and, whether *Silladar* or *non-Silladar*, have to pay him for his services.

The Non-Commissioned Officers and men in the *non-Silladar* Cavalry receive special allowances (*batta*), ranging from 6s. 8d. (Rs. 5) to 2s. (Rs. 1/8) per month, while on field or foreign (including Colonial) service. They can earn the Indian Order of Merit, and are then paid an allowance according to their rank and the class of the Order of Merit that has been awarded them for their gallantry.

Of the 137 regiments composing the Indian Infantry, some of them have a larger number of officers and men than others. The smaller ones are recruited in the Madras Presidency, and consist of 613 officers and men, of whom thirteen are British and sixteen Indian officers, and the rest (584) Indian Non-Commissioned Officers and men. The larger ones, recruited in the remaining portions of the Peninsula, have 927 units, fifteen of whom are British, and sixteen Indian Officers, and 896 Indian Non-Commissioned Officers and men. A few Infantry regiments, for instance, those of Gurkhas, are composed of two battalions each, with a double complement of officers and men.

The organization of the Infantry regiment is similar to that of the Cavalry. The names of officers, in some instances, however, are different. Thus, the senior Indian Officer is styled the *Subadar Major*. The company commanders are called *Subadars*. The Sergeants are known as *Havildars*.

The *Subadar* Major is paid, in the Indian Infantry, £6 13s. 4d. (Rs. 100), and £3 6s. 8d. (Rs. 50) a month in addition, for assisting the Commandant.

The *Subadar* also is paid £6 13s. 4d. (Rs. 100).

The */cmadar* is paid £3 6s. 8d. (Rs. 50).

Officers doing "extra duty" receive additional pay. For instance, one who is acting as "Indian Adjutant" is given £1 3s. 4d. (Rs. 17/8/-) in addition to his regular pay.

The Indian Infantry Officers, like those of the Cavalry, are admitted into the "Order of British India," and the "Indian Order of Merit," and receive allowances according to fixed scales.

The Non-Commissioned Officer of highest rank in the Infantry is the *Havildar* or Sergeant. He is paid £1 4s. od. (Rs. 18).

If he acts as *Havildar* Major (Sergeant-Major), or Pay Quartermaster *Havildar*, he receives 6s. 8d. (Rs. 5), in some cases 7s. (Rs. 5/4/-) more. If he acts as Orderly he receives an additional 2s. 5 5-6d. (Rs. 1/13/10.)

Next to the *Havildar* comes the *Naik* (Corporal), who receives £1 1s. 4d. (Rs. 16). If he is a Drill *Naik* he receives 3s. 4d. (Rs. 2/8/-), in some cases 4s. 8d. (Rs. 3/8/-) extra.

Below the *Naik* is the Drummer and Bugler, who draws 14s. 8d. (Rs. 11), and is paid 6s. 8d. (Rs. 5) extra, if he acts as Drum-Major.

The Sepoy (private) is given 14s. 8d. (Rs. 11).

Infantry non-commissioned officers and men who show uncommon bravery are awarded one or the other of the three classes of the "Indian Order of Merit," according to the nature of their daring deeds, and this brings them a small additional allowance.

All Infantry officers and men receive field allowances (*batta*). while on active service, ranging from £1 0s. 0d. (Rs. 15) to 6s. 8d. (Rs. 5).

Whether officer or private, and no matter to what branch of the Army he may belong, the field allowance of an Indian soldier usually begins when he leaves his cantonment and ends when he returns to his station. A few to whom this rule does not apply receive their *batta* at all times and in all circumstances, except when absent on leave, etc.

The Indian Infantry regiments serving in

Burma, Assam, Sind, and outside India are given "local allowances." In the case of Burma, the *Subadar* Major receives £3 6s. 8d (Rs. 50), and the Sepoy 8s. (Rs. 6) extra under this head, and the ranks in between are given allowances graded proportionately.

It is interesting to note that, recently, four battalions of Indian Infantry and a mountain battery were stationed at Hong Kong; two battalions were at Singapore; the same number were in Ceylon; one battalion was serving in North China; another was in the Persian Gulf; and five Infantry regiments were employed by the Imperial Government on Colonial garrison duty. A Cavalry regiment was strengthening the Consular Guards in Southern Persia.

In order to serve in the Infantry, a recruit must be five feet four inches high. This rule, however, is relaxed in the case of the Gurkhas, who are accepted if five feet tall. The chest measurement must be at least 32 inches, and the requirements range from that up to 36 inches, according to the height and age of the recruit, the latter figure being the standard for a man twenty-five years old, and over five feet ten inches in height.

The ranks and pays in the other branches of the Army are similar to those already noted, and may be left out. The composition, being different, may be outlined:

A Mountain Battery consists of 331 officers and men, of whom five are British and three Indian Officers, and the rest Indian Non-Commissioned Officers and men.

A Frontier Garrison Artillery Company comprises six officers (three British and three Indian), and 272 Indian Non-Commissioned Officers and men, or 278 in all.

A company of Sappers and Miners has 196 officers and men, of whom two are British and three are Indian Officers, and two are British Non-Commissioned Officers, and the remainder are Indian Non-Commissioned Officers and men.

The strength of a military railway company is 198 officers and men, of whom two (one commissioned and one non-commissioned) Officers are British, and the rest are Indian—three Officers, and 193 Non-Commissioned Officers and men.

The pensions received by retired Indian officers and men are very small. The table on page 122, abstracted from *Army Regulations of India*, Vol. I., page 204, gives an idea of the sums that are paid them:

The Indian Army Reservist who has served for twenty-five years, including "five years' colour and embodied service, which latter does not include any period during which Reservists are attached to units for training," receives from 4s. (Rs. 3) to 6s. 8d. (Rs. 5) a month.

Pensions granted to those invalided before they have served their full time are much smaller. Particulars concerning them have to be omitted in the interests of space.

Indian officers and men are given pensions

Rank.	Service.	Rate of Pension p.m. £ s. d.	Rs.
Sowars, sepoys, others ranking as such, etc.	After 18 years.	0 5 4	4.0.0
Lance-daffadars, *naiks*, others ranking as such, and trumpeters of Indian Cavalry	,, 18 ,,	0 6 8	5.0.0
	,, 21 ,,	0 9 4	7.0.0
Daffadars, *havildars*, others ranking as such, farrier majors, and *salutris* of *Silladar* Cavalry, drum-, trumpet-, fife-, and bugle majors, *salutris* of artillery, etc.	,, 18 ,,	0 9 4	7.0.0
	,, 21 ,,	0 10 8	8.0.0
	,, 24 ,,	0 12 0	9.0.0
Jemadars	,, 20 ,,	1 1 4	16.0.0
	,, 24 ,,	1 6 8	20.0.0
Risaldar-majors, *subadar*-majors, *risaldars*, *ressaidars*, or *subadars* ...	,, 21 ,,	2 0 0	30.0.0
	,, 24 ,,	2 6 8	35.0.0
	,, 28 ,,	2 13 4	40.0.0
	,, 32 ,,	3 6 8	50.0.0

In the case of *risaldar*-majors and *subadar*-majors, the rates of pension mentioned are exclusive of the personal allowance of Rs. 50 p.m. . . . which still will be continued, or granted, to them after they are pensioned.

for wounds and injuries received while on service. The highest is granted to Indian commissioned officers above the rank of *Jemadar* employed in most of the regiments. They receive £1 13s. 4d. (Rs. 25) per mensem for each wound, and £1 4s. od. (Rs. 18) per mensem for each injury. The private who has been thirty-two years in the service receives 14s. 8d. (Rs. 11) per mensem for a wound adjudged to fall in the first class. There is a regular scale, graduated according to the term of service and the nature of the wound, until the minimum, or 3s. 3d. (Rs. 2/7/0) for an injury of the fourth class suffered by a Sepoy or *Sowar*, who has served under fifteen years, is reached.

The families of Indian combatants who are "killed in action or die from wounds received in action within six months of being wounded, or from sickness contracted or accident received while on foreign service," are entitled to pensions regulated according to different scales. The highest is £2 8s. od.

(Rs. 36), paid to the heirs of a *Risaldar*, *Ressaidar*, *Subadar*, etc. The lowest is paid to the heirs of men of the Indian Submarine Mining Corps, who receive 3s. 2d. (Rs. 2/6/0) a month. In nearly all cases these pensions are bestowed for certain specified terms of years. In the case of males under six years old, for instance, they cease when the recipient reaches the age of eighteen. Males over six years old and under fifty receive the pensions for a period of twelve years. Males over fifty enjoy the grants for life, as do also females of any age.

This brief outline of the military resources of British India may be concluded with a few words regarding the expenditure that India annually incurs in keeping up this organization. The net outlay on the Army during 1912-13 totalled £18,348,723. This amount did not include the sum incurred in building military and special defence works, which alone amounted to £824,484. In addition, India contributed £392,259 towards the expenses of His Majesty's ships employed in the Indian seas. In other words, the Indian taxpayers paid £19,565,466[7] for the maintenance of the Armies.

Having described the "Native" Army of British India, I may now refer to the Army in the employ of the Rajas. These are of two kinds:

1. The ordinary armies maintained by the Rajas, consisting of 161,000 soldiers, or 214,000 strong, if the 47,000 armed police kept by the Indian Rulers are included; and

2. The Imperial Service Troops, consisting of 22,271 officers and men.

To describe them in order:

In writing of the ordinary armies employed by the Rajas, it is customary to add together the soldiery in the service of all of them except that of the Ruler of Nepal. The latest edition of the Imperial Gazetteer of India, *The Indian Empire*, Vol. IV., says:

7. *Statement exhibiting the Moral and Material Progress and Condition of India, 1912-13*, pp. 127, 128.

> " . . . the Native States maintain, according to their position, large or small bodies of soldiers as local military forces. These number collectively about 16,000 cavalry, 7,000 artillery, and 70,000 infantry, or 93,000 in all, with many guns; . . ."

and then continues:

> "A few words may be added about the Nepal . . . armies. The Nepal army consists of about 45,000 men, regular and irregular, including 2,500 artillery, with about 900 guns; . . ."[8]

The strength mentioned in each case is that of the armies as they existed prior to 1909, when the work was issued. The latest figures are supplied by the *Statement Exhibiting the Moral and Material Progress and Conditions of India during the Year 1911-12, and the Nine Preceding Years,* according to which the military forces maintained by the Native States amount to about

8. Pp. 375, 376.

111,000 men (besides some 47,000 armed police).[9] The total strength of the Nepal Army is now said to be about 50,000.

The separation of the armies of Nepal from those of the other Rajas is merely technical, and I have ignored it in considering the subject.

It is not possible to supply details concerning the division of the armies employed by the various Rajas into Artillery, Cavalry, Infantry, etc. The figures extracted from the *Imperial Gazetteer*, though antiquated, give a rough idea of such divisions.

Great diversity of opinion prevails regarding the efficiency of the Rajas' Armies. Some authorities openly declare that this force is not worth very much. Others, on the contrary, maintain that at least some of the troops employed by the important Rajas are good fighters, well drilled, and capable of giving a good account of themselves under all conditions. Others again merely aver that the

9. P. 15.

soldiery contains capital material, which needs much training to make it capable of engaging on equal terms with any modern Army.

I do not feel competent to settle these disputes authoritatively, but certain it is that during recent years some of the Indian Rulers have, with the greatest patience, mastered military tactics, obtaining instruction from European experts, and have worked indefatigably to improve the morale of their army. Others have imported into their service highly qualified men to bring the efficiency of their troops up to modern requirements. It may be asserted dogmatically that all this energy has not been expended in vain, but has resulted in improving the fighting qualities of the armies maintained by the Rajas presiding over the large, and even some of the small, Indian States.

Concerning the efficiency of the other branch of armies in the service of Indian Rulers, namely, the Imperial Service Troops, there is no difference of opinion. Indians and

Photo by G. T. Jones & Son, Kingston-on-Thames.

OFFICERS OF IMPERIAL SERVICE TROOPS BELONGING TO THE RULERS OF PATIALA, JIND, NABHA, KAPURTHALA, BAHAWALPUR AND MALER KOTLA, ALL PUNJAB STATES.

British authorities alike have nothing but the highest praise for the splendid type of manhood that goes into its composition, the excellent armament and equipment with which the soldiers are provided, the up-to-date training they receive, and the efficiency they acquire.

The Imperial Service Troops were constituted comparatively recently, and a word may be said regarding their history. In the 80's, when a Russian attack on the North-West Frontier was deemed imminent, the late Nizam of Hyderabad, his Highness Mir Mahbub Ali Shah Bahadur, G.C.S.I., placed his sword at the disposal of the British, and offered to contribute a large sum of money (£400,000, or sixty lakhs of rupees) to help the British Indian Government. Other Rajas followed suit. The alarm proved to be unfounded, but the Administration began to work out a scheme of Imperial defence in which Rajas could co-operate.

As the project finally matured, the Indian

States were allowed to volunteer to set apart portions of their troops, or raise new corps, which would be armed, equipped and trained the same as the "Native" Army in British India, and which the State could place at the disposal of the British Indian Government during times of necessity. In such eventuality these troops were to be federated with British Indian forces, and were to be under the orders of the Commander-in-Chief in India. The British Indian Government undertook to appoint and maintain the requisite staff to advise the Rajas concerning the training of these special troops, and to inspect them periodically so that their efficiency might be maintained at the highest possible level.

By 1903, Imperial Service Troops were maintained by the States of:

Alwar,	Bikaner,
Bahawalpur,	Faridkot,
Bharatpur,	Gwalior,
Bhavnagar,	Hyderabad,
Bhopal,	Indore,

Jaipur,	Mysore,
Jind,	Nabha,
Jodhpur,	Navanagar,
Junagarh,	Patiala,
Kapurthala,	Rampur,
Kashmir,	and
Maler Kotla,	Sirmur.

On 1st April, 1912, the number of States employing these troops had risen to twenty-nine, and the strength exceeded 22,000 officers and men. The composition of the force then was, roughly:

Infantry	10,000
Cavalry	7,500
Transport Corps ...	2,700
Camel Corps ...	700
Sappers and Miners	700

It is important to note that the State of Gwalior furnished 4,000, Kashmir and Jammu 3,500, and Patiala, Hyderabad, and Alwar over 1,000 officers and men each.

The Imperial Service Troops have already taken part in the following campaigns:

The Bikaner Infantry fought in Somaliland in 1903.

The Alwar Infantry, the Bikaner Infantry, the Jodhpur Lancers, and the Maler Kotla Sappers accompanied the China Expeditionary Field Force in 1900-01.

The Jind Infantry, the Nabha Infantry, the 1st Patiala Infantry, the Jodhpur Lancers, the Kapurthala Lancers, the Kashmir Mountain Batteries, the Sirmur Sappers, the Maler Kotla Sappers, and the Jaipur and Gwalior Transport Corps took part in the North-West Frontier Expeditions of 1897-98 and 1895.

The 1st and 2nd Kashmir Infantry and the No. 1 Kashmir Mountain Battery engaged in the Hunza Nagar campaign of 1891.

The Kashmir Mountain Batteries have helped in relieving the Gilgit garrison.

The European war conflict demonstrated that it is no delusion on the part of any writer to reckon the forces employed by the various Indian Rulers, almost 700 in number, as a part of the strength on which the British can depend in critical times. Each Raja who possessed any Imperial Service Troops or other soldiery rushed forward immediately upon finding that Great Britain was sure to be involved, to tender his army to his Suzerain; and many of them offered, in addition, large contributions of money, and even their personal treasures.

The Nizam of Hyderabad (his Highness Nizam-ul-Mulk Nizam-ud-Daula, Nawab Mir Sir Usman Ali Khan Bahadur, G.C.S.I.), who is Hon. Colonel of the 20th Deccan Horse, was among the first to offer his military resources, and has given £400,000 (Rs. 6,000,000) to be used in fighting the foes of the Empire.

The Maharaja of Mysore (his Highness Maharaja Sri Sir Krishnaraja Wodiyar Bahadur, G.C.S.I.), Hon. Colonel of the 26th King George's Own Light Cavalry (Indian Army), not content with giving his soldiers to fight for the honour and glory of the King-Emperor, also contributed £333,333 (Rs. 5,000,000) to the war fund.

The Prime Minister of Nepal and its *de facto* Ruler (his Highness Maharaja Sir Chandra Shamsher Jang, Rana Bahadur, G.C.B., G.C.V.O., G.C.S.I., D.C.L.), Hon. Colonel of the 4th Gurkha Rifles, placed the Army of Nepal at the disposal of the Government of India to be used in the European war, and in addition gave £22,000 (Rs. 330,000) for equipping Gurkha soldiers belonging to his own race serving in British regiments with machine guns and other requisites.

The Maharaja-Gaekwar of Baroda (his Highness Shri Sir Sayaji Rao III., G.C.S.I.), placed all his resources, military and otherwise, at the disposal of His Majesty.

The Maharaja of Gwalior (his Highness Maharaja Sir Madho Rao Sindhia Bahadur, G.C.S.I., G.C.V.O., LL.D., A.D.C.), Hon. Major-General, Hon. Colonel 1st Duke of York's Own Lancers, or "Skinner's Horse" (Indian Army), besides offering his Imperial

Service Troops, undertook to provide thousands of remounts, and in conjunction with the Ruler of Bhopal (her Highness Nawab Sultan Jahan Begum, G.C.S.I., G.C.I.E., C.I.), and other Rajas, fitted out a hospital ship, "The Loyalty," to transport wounded soldiers to hospitals. He also gave large sums of money to be used in various ways.

The Maharaja of Jammu and Kashmir (his Highness Sir Partap Singh Bahadur, G.C.S.I., G.C.I.E.), Hon. Major-General, Hon. Colonel 37th Dogras, besides lending his Imperial Service Troops and all his resources, provided transportation facilities and entertainment for British troops passing through his territories.

The Maharaja of Rewa (his Highness Sri Sir Venkat Raman Singh Bahadur, G.C.S.I.), outdid all the rest, and included his personal ornaments in his gift to the Empire.

These are but a few names that I have singled out of some 700, all of whom, with truly kingly generosity, contributed to the fighting forces, to the war chest, and to the relief funds. It is striking that in the list should be Rulers whose States are so widely separated as those of Las Bela, Kalat, and Kashmir in the North-West, Sikkim, Tibet, Cooch Behar and Manipur in the North-East, and Travancore in Southern India.

Not a few of the Rajas and their kinsfolk and nobles volunteered to fight in person.

Among the number who actually came to the battlefield were two, the Maharaja of Bikaner and his Highness Maharaja Sir Partab Singhji, G.C.V.O., G.C.S.I., K.C.B., LL.D., Hon. A.D.C. to H.M. the King-Emperor, Hon. Maj.-Gen. (British Army), Hon. Col. 34th Horse (Indian Army), Hon. Commandant of the Imperial Cadet Corps, who had rendered valiant service in fighting Britain's enemies.

Two more, the Maharaja of Patiala[10] (his

10. As this volume is going to press news has been cabled that his Highness has been compelled by illness to return to India from Aden.

Highness Maharaja-dhiraja Sri Sir Bhupindar Singh Mahindar Bahadur, G.C.I.E.), and Prince Hitindra Narayan, a younger brother of the present Maharaja of Cooch Behar (his Highness Jitindra Narayan Bhup), are the sons of Rulers who fought for the British.

One of the Rajas, the Maharaja of Jodhpur (his Highness Maharaja-dhiraja Sumer Singh Bahadur), was only a youth, being in his seventeenth years.

The Maharaja of Kishengarh (Major his Highness Maharaja-dhiraja Sir Madan Singh Bahadur, K.C.S.I., K.C.I.E.), who also came to the Continent with the expeditionary force from India, was thirty years old, being four years younger than the Ruler of Ratlam (his Highness Raja Sir Sajjan Singh, K.C.S.I.), Major 39th Horse (Indian Army), who also came over.

In addition to these Hindu and Sikh Rajas and Princes, several Musalman Rulers and their relatives, among them the Nawab of Maler Kotla (his Highness Ahmud Ali

Khan, Bahadur), the Nawab of Sachin (Lieut. his Highness Sidi Ibrahim Mahomed Yakub Khan, A.D.C.), and the son and heir of her Highness the Begum of Bhopal (Major Sahebzada Nawab Muhammad Nasrulla Khan), of the 9th Bhopal Infantry, proceeded to the Continent to fight for the King-Emperor.

It may be added that his Highness Aga Sultan Mahomed Shah, G.C.I.E., G.C.S.I., Hon. LL.D., Cambridge, the Aga Khan, who is not the Ruler of any State, but is a lineal descendant of the Prophet Mahomed, and is the religious leader of millions of Musalmans, offered to serve even as a private to fight for the King-Emperor.

To sum up:

Putting the forces employed by the Rajas together with those held in fee by British India, Hindostan has a standing Army of over 420,000, namely, the "Native" Armies in British India, 162,000; the European Army, 75,573; the Armies of the Rajas,

Photo by courtesy of his Highness.

TROOPS OF HIS HIGHNESS THE THAKORE SAHEB OF GONDAL.

161,000; and the Rajas' Imperial Service Troops, 22,000.

In addition to this standing Army are auxiliary forces amounting to 119,382, namely, the Military Police, etc., of British India, 35,000; the Volunteers, 37,382; and the Rajas' Armed Police, 47,000.

Over and above these are the officers and men on the Reserve list, whose enrolled strength on 1st April, 1912, was 37,382.

Thus, altogether, India has 580,000 men ready to fight its own or its Suzerain's enemies at any moment.

Need I add that, if necessary, the fighting clans of Ind can officer and man this strength many times over?

CHAPTER IV.

Deeds of Dash and Daring.

IT would take volumes to describe the nonchalant manner in which the Indian fighter faces danger, conquers seemingly unsurmountable difficulties, braves privations, and wins success, or dies like a hero. All that can be attempted here is to relate a few stray incidents which have occurred during recent campaigns in which the Indian soldiers have taken part, to throw a light on the way they fight for Britain.

During the Tibet campaign of 1904 Labh Singh, *Havildar* or Sergeant in the 32nd Sikh Pioneers, learned that a box of guncotton was hidden about a hundred and fifty yards from his post at Palla—a little village. Undeterred by the volleys that the enemy directed against him, he rushed out alone to where the box lay and tried to lift it and carry it back with him. But the gun-cotton was much too heavy for him to manage single-handed. He, therefore, once more braved the hail of lead and ran back across the open space to Palla. Dragging some companions-in-arms along with him, he again made for the box. The Sikhs, between them, were able to lift it up, and returned to Palla bearing it in triumph.[1]

As if it was not enough for him to expose himself four times to the Tibetans' guns in performing this exploit, a few hours afterwards Labh Singh laid five mines, with bullets flying about him all the time.[2]

While serving in the same campaign a Sikh officer, Wasawa Singh, *Subadar* or Indian Captain in the same infantry regiment, turned the tide of battle at the Karola on May 6th, 1904. The Tibetans had taken

1. *Regimental History of the 32nd Sikh Pioneers*, by H. R. Brander, Vol. II., p. 58.

2. *Ibid.*, p. 58.

a stand behind a fortress perched on the crest of a cliff 18,000 feet above the level of the sea, the highest point for miles around, where they completely blocked the progress of the advancing British force. It was necessary to drive the enemy from their strong position. But this meant climbing up a cliff of slippery shale, which offered practically no foothold, exposed all the time to the fire from the Tibetan guns. Wasawa Singh led a small band of his men up the side of the mountain, and unexpectedly attacked the fortress from behind, in its only vulnerable point. So terrified were the Tibetans at finding the enemy right upon them when they had considered their fortress impregnable, that all they could think of doing was to run for their lives, leaving behind them their arms and ammunition. The final result of the brave *Subadar's* coup was that the enemy retired from their main position, leaving the attacking forces in possession of the point of vantage.[3]

3. *Ibid.*, pp. 28—38.

Thirteen days later—on May 19th—a small detachment of the 8th Gurkhas accomplished a thrilling exploit. Very early in the morning, before the dark night-sky became streaked with grey, the party crept out of their post near Gyantse and surrounded a building a short distance from it that had been occupied by the enemy. Not until the storming force began to fire upon them did the Tibetans realize that they were in danger. Then they hastily scrambled up to the roof and fired their rifles and hurled stones and bricks at their foes. Hearing the noise of the shooting, the Tibetan fortress some distance away turned all its large muskets on the Gurkhas and swept the whole neighbourhood with leaden and copper balls. The invaders hugged the walls of the building, while some Sikh miners crept around to the back of it and forced a breach by exploding gun-cotton against it. The occupants, sixty in number, were taken utterly by surprise by this simultaneous attack from front and rear, and completely lost their heads. Twenty of them, on hearing the explosion and the crash of the falling wall, jumped out and tried to run away to the fortress in the village. The Sikh soldiers anticipating such an exodus were prepared for it, and immediately killed ten of the fleeing men. The Gurkhas, meanwhile, streamed in through the breach the moment it was made and put to death all who were inside. Only ten out of the sixty who had been in possession of the house before the attack were alive when the sun rose a few minutes later.[4]

The Gurkhas remained in the place to hold it as a post, and for a long time worked to repair and fortify it, under a constant fire, night and day, from the fortress in the town near by.[5]

In the course of the operations in China directed against the Boxers during 1900-01, Tura Baz Khan, *Subadar* in the 20th

4. *Ibid.*, pp. 40—43.
5. *Ibid.*, p. 42.

Infantry, or Brownlow's Punjabis, now Hon. Capt. *Sardar Bahadur* (Valiant Chief), Hon. A.D.C. to his Excellency the Commander-in-Chief in India (Sir Beauchamp Duff, G.C.B., K.C.S.I., K.C.V.O., C.I.E.), showed that an Indian soldier does not permit himself to be led astray by tempting bribes. He was informed by a Chinese co-religionist that if he would search the garden surrounding a certain house in Kaiping, and a temple not far from it, he would find a large store of arms and ammunition hidden there. Without informing anyone of his intention, he quietly proceeded to explore the site. He lighted upon a veritable armoury—150 rifles and three batteries of Krupp field guns complete for action except for the breech blocks, which had been removed, and 300 rounds of ammunition and shell for each of them. The Chinese authorities offered the Indian officer as much silver as he and his men could carry away with them if they would refrain from reporting the discovery to their superior, and leave the guns where they had found them. But the *Subadar* and his companions indignantly spurned the bribe, and carried away the spoils. A semi-official chronicle of the event relates that Tura Baz Khan's find greatly chagrined the Germans garrisoned in the place, who resented the fact that the soldiers from Hindostan, under their very noses, had been able to carry out such a brilliant coup.[6]

While detachments of sappers and miners, cavalry, infantry, and a mountain battery were storming the massive, mud-walled Fort Nodiz, occupying a strong position commanding the Turbat-Tump road, in Baluchistan, on December 20th, 1901, Hamid Khan, *Subadar* in the 27th Baluch Light Infantry, two sappers, and two British officers led a party into the fort under the hot fire of Mahomed Ali Khan's band of outlaws, 90 strong. A hand-to-hand fight with his swordsmen ensued. These men were soon driven

6. *History of the 20th Infantry (Brownlow's Punjabis)*, pp. 105, 106.

back, but rifle shots from the towers of the surrounding walls laid low the two Lieutenants and several of the Indians. A number of inexperienced soldiers had accompanied the *Subadar*. On seeing their officers and comrades wounded, they stampeded back through the breach to their lines. But Hamid Khan and the two sappers picked up the fallen Lieutenants and men, and carried them to safety. Reinforced, they once again rushed forward, took the reduits by bayonet charge, blew up the fortress, and killed or made prisoners all the outlaws, including their leader.[7]

In the capture of Dargai during the Tirah campaign of 1897, Gurkhas and Sikhs, fighting side by side with Gordons, Derbys, and Dorsets, showed contempt for the enemy's fire, such as has seldom been witnessed on the battlefield. So far as the British could discern, the peak of the high cliff, whose

7. *Historical Records of the 127th Baluch Light Infantry*, pp. 146—162 and 164.

natural position rendered it proof against cannon-balls, shells, and shrapnels, had been chosen by the tribesmen to form their stronghold, and could be reached only by a single path, so narrow that two men could hardly squeeze through it side by side, and so difficult that the ascent could only be made very slowly. The shrewd frontiersmen had built encircling walls, with loopholes pointing downwards, so cleverly constructed that every inch of the path for the fifty yards or more that were exposed to their fire could be raked with their bullets. It seemed that no mortal foe could face such a hail of lead, and forge forward to take the fortress. The Gurkhas, with the Dorsets behind them, however, proceeded up the mountain, two by two. The enemy's bullets ruthlessly mowed them down, but by sheer doggedness a few managed to make their way across the exposed part of the path, and take refuge in a position where they were safe from the fire of the tribesmen within the fort. A lull followed, and then the rest of the Gurkhas, the Sikhs, the Derbys, the Dorsets, and the Gordons, once again rushed across. Men fell at every step till the path was practically choked with the dead and dying. Not a few Indian and British soldiers stopped on their way to carry their wounded comrades out of the death belt, and lost their lives in the attempt at rescue. The rush did not relax until sufficient numbers had joined the advance party of Gurkhas to take the fortress by main force. When the tribesmen noticed this, they fled helter skelter down the mountain side by a back exit known only to themselves, not daring to stand up against foes who could face the deadly fire that had been poured down upon them from the heights above.[8]

The expeditionary force of Indians sent in 1897 to Mombasa, British East Africa, to quell a stubborn mutiny in the Uganda Protectorate, distinguished itself by facing

8. *The Indian Frontier War, 1897*, by Lionel James, pp. 114—123.

heavy odds that would have daunted less brave souls. The climate was most trying, even to those inured to the heat of the tropics. The privations caused by short rations, lack of transport facilities, and the difficult nature of the country they were called upon to traverse, were almost beyond human endurance. On October 9th and 10th, 1898, a small company told off to act as the rear and baggage guards of a detachment that was pursuing the Soudanese mutineers was set upon by overwhelming numbers of the enemy. They stood their ground so valiantly that every one of those who survived were given the Indian Order of Merit for their "gallantry and devotion," to use the words of the Order of the Government of India, bestowing the honour upon them.[9]

During the Mohmand Campaign of 1897, a company of Afridis of Brownlow's Punjabis refused to wait to fill their empty water bottles

9. *Historical Records of the 127th Baluch Light Infantry*, pp. 104—139.

or partake of food on coming into camp from picquet duty, which had lasted throughout the night, so anxious were they to march upon the enemy. Hungry and thirsty as they were, they climbed up several thousand feet over a precipitous mountain, and for full fourteen hours engaged the foe, not thinking of their aching, empty stomachs and parched throats, until they had scored an unqualified victory.[10]

In the same year a garrison of privates of the 36th Sikhs, only twenty-one in number all told, occupying a tiny, wooden-doored, mud block-house, lost their lives at Saraghari, a small signalling post on the Samana range in the North-West Frontier Province, after keeping a force of nearly 8,000 Orakzais at bay for six and a half hours. Not until every one of them had been killed were the fanatic tribesmen able to break into the little fort. Two memorials have been erected in honour of the brave band, one at Ferozepore, the

10. *History of the 20th Infantry*, p. 95; also *The Indian Frontier War*, pp. 60, 61.

home of the soldiers who laid down their lives on the altar of duty, and the other at Amritsar, their religious capital; and it is noteworthy that a portion of the funds for these monuments was subscribed by appreciative British comrades in arms and European civilians.[11]

The relief of Chitral, in 1895, strikingly demonstrated the Indian soldier's ability to adjust himself to conditions diametrically opposite to those to which he has been accustomed from his birth. Men of the Punjab plains waded through snow from three to five feet deep, and so soft that they often sank up to their arm-pits in the drift. The glare was so trying that many of them were snow-blinded, even though they wore tinted glasses. In the Himalayan mid-winter they had to traverse mountain country, one pass (the Shandur), which they crossed, being 12,230 feet high. They often had to go without food and had little water to drink. Even when

11. Indian newspapers for September, 1897; also *Encyclopædia Britannica*, Eleventh Edition, Vol. XXIV., p. 203.

exposed to the heaviest fire they continued to advance. A Sikh private—Ishar Singh—although suffering from such a serious wound in his leg that eventually it had to be amputated, stubbornly refused to permit himself to be carried to the rear by the bearer corps, but gallantly kept on fighting, until he swooned from loss of blood. Hungry and thirsty, and tired almost beyond human endurance though they were, they eagerly volunteered to rush strongly guarded villages at the end of a day's marching and fighting, and cheerfully went to and fro carrying their wounded comrades and precious ammunition to places of safety.[12]

One engagement especially showed the cool nerve of the Indian gunners belonging to a detachment of the mountain battery in the employ of the Indian State of Kashmir and Jammu. Exposed to heavy fire directed by the frontiersmen from three sides, from

12. *History of the Imperial Service Troops of Native States*, by S. Beatson, pp. 141—144; also *Regimental History of the 32nd Sikh Pioneers*, Vol. I., pp. 148—175.

natural positions of the greatest vantage, they constantly kept shifting the direction and range of their guns to fire at rapidly changing distances, in obedience to the commands of their superiors. So plucky were they that two of them, badly wounded, one in the hand, the other in the groin, kept on firing without mentioning their injuries, until they became senseless from pain and exhaustion.[13]

In another frontier campaign, a Musalman soldier furnished a touching example of how the Indian fighter's word can be relied upon, and how he is devoted heart and soul to duty. Just as Major Brownlow had received orders to march against the rebel North-West frontiersmen, one of the privates came to him and begged for a few days' leave, urging that if he was not allowed to go he could not be married on the appointed date, and as long as he lived he would be the laughing stock of everyone who knew him. He promised to rejoin his company at a certain point on the march

13. *History of the Imperial Service Troops, etc.*, p. 143.

Photo by G. T. Jones & Son, Kingston-on-Thames.

A DETACHMENT OF MOUNTAIN BATTERIES. MIXED RACES.

on a given day. Knowing that the man was trustworthy and would keep his word, Major Brownlow allowed him to go. He joined his regiment just in the nick of time, as the battle was about to begin. Hurrying into his uniform, he proceeded at once to hunt for his Commandant, and found him in "The Eagle's Nest." Without speaking a word, he saluted his superior officer and began loading his rifle, but before he could bring it to his shoulder and take aim at the enemy, a bullet struck him squarely in the centre of the forehead, and his career both as a soldier and a benedict was brought to a tragic end.[14]

During the Third Burmese War of 1885-87, Indian officers and men distinguished themselves in hunting down and killing or capturing bands of desperate outlaws who had taken to the thick, virgin forests.

Early in the campaign Arsala Khan—a *Jemadar* or Indian Lieutenant in the regiment now known as the 127th Queen Mary's Own

14. *History of the 20th Infantry*, pp. 118, 119.

Baluch Light Infantry—volunteered to lead a party of his regiment through dense jungle near Tathwe, in Upper Burma. Single-handed he attacked a picquet consisting of three of the enemy's men, whom he took by surprise, killing one and putting the other two to flight.[15]

Some time later Aziz Khan, another *Jemadar*, commanding a company of mounted men, alone charged groups of Red Karens at Nga-Kiang, rescuing from them two of his troopers who had fallen wounded in the mélée, and killing three of the foe.[16]

In the same engagement Alladad Khan, a *Lance Naik*, or Lance Corporal, in command of a half section of mounted soldiers, pursued the Red Karens, and attacked a body of them hiding in the bed of a stream. He was entirely alone and under heavy fire, but when they ran away from him and sought safety in a bamboo grove, he

15. *Historical Records of the 127th Baluch Light Infantry*, pp. 70, 71.
16. *Ibid.*, p. 71.

continued to harass them until he drove them away.[17]

A Baluchi private, Khaim Khan, in the same brush with the Karens, attacked several bodies of them single-handed while exposed to the enemy's bullets, and did not desist until he had routed them, even though he had been seriously wounded in the encounter.[18]

The Brahman soldiers covered themselves with glory during this Burma campaign. The sepoys of the 11th Bengal Infantry were the first to set foot within the fort at the storming of Minhla. On another occasion a detachment of the 4th Bengal Infantry, commanded by a Brahman *Subadar*, made a forced march of sixty-five miles in a day and a half, and immediately upon arriving at their destination, took Kendat by storm and saved the lives of many British officials who had been condemned to a cruel death.[19]

17. *Ibid.*, p. 71.
18. *Ibid.*, pp. 71, 72.
19. *Handbooks for the Indian Army: Brahmans*, by Captain A. H. Bingley and Captain A. Nicholls, p. 10.

The Abyssinian campaign of 1867-68 furnished splendid opportunities for the Indian fighter to show his versatility. A thousand mules had been landed without drivers, and were roaming about at large. The Indians were at once detailed to collect them into paddocks, and did so with great difficulty. Later on they were told off to construct the famous Zula Pass over the Devil's Staircase. The fate of the Abyssinian campaign -largely rested on it, for without this roadway the British army would have been blocked in its progress to the heart of the rebellious King Theodore's country. The Indians proved equal to the occasion, and finished the arduous task in a little over six weeks. They travelled three hundred miles by a forced march, carrying their own kits throughout their long journey, as no transport facilities were at hand, and joined headquarters before Magdala. They were just a little too late to take part in the Arogee action, but were keen to engage in battle although footsore and tired to the point of exhaustion from their long tramp through an arid district, on short rations and with insufficient water.[20]

A dramatic instance showing how the Indian fighter can defy the enemy was furnished in 1863, while the British were engaged in punishing the wild men of the North-West Frontier. The enemy all at once sued for a respite and suggested that a song would help to beguile the night's fighting. One of them, a Bajauri lad, sang a bellicose lay of his clan. As the last strains of his martial melody died away, two Afridis belonging to the British side stepped from behind the breastworks, mounted the wall, and sat nonchalantly dangling their legs, their figures standing out boldly in the bright moonlight. They replied to the Bajauri's song by singing one of their own, the burden of which was contempt for their foes. As the last words rang out, the two men hastily

20. *Historical Records of the 127th Baluch Light Infantry*, pp. 15—19.

jumped behind the parapet and fighting was instantaneously resumed with renewed fierceness.[21]

During the same campaign Maula Dad Khan, then a *Jemadar* in the 1st Punjab Infantry, settled the fate of two of the enemy, who for some time had been annoying the British forces by firing on their camp at night. When asked by his Captain what could be done to silence the "snipers," he quietly replied by slipping over the edge of the cliff on which the camp was pitched. After a considerable interval two shots were heard, and a few minutes later he came back bringing the head-gear and arms of his fallen foes as witnesses of his deed. He had traced the hiding place of the enemy by the flashes of their guns, crept up to them and killed them.[22]

The Indian soldier's deeds of daring so fill the pages of the annals chronicling the events of the Sepoy Mutiny of 1857, that one

21. *History of the 20th Infantry*, pp. 115, 116.
22. *Ibid.*, p. 119.

is bewildered in choosing instances of outstanding bravery. Here are a few:

Early in the course of this, probably the greatest struggle that the British have had to go through in the East, three companies of Mazbi (or Mazbee) Sikhs, each consisting of eighty men, were raised to take part in the siege of Delhi. These raw recruits were given arms and ammunition, but they were not provided with uniforms, bedding, tents, transport, or enough of anything to meet their needs. Most of them were not supplied with socks or boots. Without grumbling, however, they went forward by double marches, from Ludhiana to Delhi, a distance of about two hundred miles, acting as the guard of a train of ammunition and treasure over a mile long. When their rearguard was attacked the Sikhs, though exhausted from their long march across the Punjab plain, fought so hard that they succeeded in saving all the ammunition and treasure.[23]

23. *Regimental History of the 32nd Sikh Pioneers*, Vol. I., pp. 3, 4.

A little later a body of these same men, two hundred strong, marched forty-two miles in eleven hours. On another occasion, during an exceedingly hot and oppressive summer night, a detachment marched forty-five miles in twelve and a quarter hours. Halts are included in both instances. In neither case was a single person left on the road.[24]

At Sirpura these men advanced for over half a mile across an open plain, and, without the help of British officers or soldiers, and with no artillery to back them, attacked four guns in position. They captured the two largest cannon, and would have taken the other two as well, but, being horsed, they managed to get away, only to be seized at some distance, by cavalry.[25]

The Mazbis actually starved during the operations about Delhi, as none of them was given any pay until the city had fallen. Then an advance of two shillings and eightpence

24. *Ibid.*, p. 192.
25. *Ibid.*, p. 194.

was doled out to the most necessitous, and not until weeks later did they receive a month's pay. But without a murmur, enduring the utmost fatigue and constantly suffering from the pangs of hunger, they stood firm by the British colours and helped the Britons master the mutineers.[26]

All that was left of three Indian regiments, the 13th, 48th, and 71st Native Infantry, behaved with noteworthy valour in defending the Lucknow Residency at the time of the Mutiny. These men were fighting so close to the rebel sepoys that they could talk with their foes between shots. The mutineers used every means in their power to persuade the "faithful few" to desert the British and swell the insurrectionists' forces. But they refused to be persuaded by promises of rich reward, cajolery, threats or imprecations to be untrue to their trust. Indeed, they tried to work even harder than their British comrades, and determined to stand their ground

26. *Ibid.*, p. 194.

come what might, and defend the Residency so long as there was life in their bodies. They dug trenches, and fought in them. They even did not hesitate to perform duties in which people of their caste were forbidden to engage. For instance, Brahmans, or men of the highest caste, belonging to the 13th regiment, did not for the fraction of a moment hesitate to pick up and deposit in other graves the rotting corpses of sepoys who had been previously buried at a spot where it was necessary to erect a battery. In thus obeying the command of their officers, they outraged the fundamental principles of their religion and society. But they acted without counting the cost.[27]

At the same place (Lucknow), Mukarrab Khan, a Moslem soldier, thrust his left arm, on which he carried a shield, between the leaves of the gate to prevent the enemy from

27. *History of the Indian Mutiny*, by Sir John William Kaye and Col. G. B. Malleson, Vol. III., pp. 326, 327; and *Official Report of the Defence of Lucknow*, from Colonel J. Inglis, quoted therein, p. 388.

closing it in the face of the British forces. When his hand was badly wounded by a sword cut, he instantly thrust his other arm through the crack in the gates, before withdrawing the one that had been injured. Almost at once his right hand was nearly severed from the wrist but he stood firm until the reinforced British troops forced the doors open and the Indian and European soldiers swarmed in.[28]

One of the heroes of the Mutiny was Gambar Singh, then a Gurkha sepoy, later Colonel *Bahadur* (brave). At Lucknow he captured three guns and killed seven mutineers, single-handed and armed only with his long, curved knife (*khukri*). He was wounded in twenty-three places, lost some of his fingers, and had one of his hands nearly cut off, but refused to give up the struggle until he had accomplished his wonderful feat of arms.[29]

28. *Forty-one Years in India*, by Field-Marshal Lord Roberts of Kandahar, Vol. I., pp. 326, 327.

29. *Notes on Goorkhas*, by Capt. Eden Vansittart, p. 72.

During the siege of Arrah, the Sikh soldiers remained true to their British comrades, and did all they could to cheer and make life bearable for them. They dug a well to provide the beseiged Europeans with drinking water. They stealthily crept out at night and brought in sheep for food. They discovered and destroyed the mine that the enemy had laid to blow up the little fortress. Hukam Singh, a *Jemadar*, was so contemptuous of the enemy's bullets that under a heavy fire he climbed to the roof and threw bricks at them, taunting them as he did so.[30]

In pondering the events that led to the outbreak of the Sepoy Mutiny, and the tribulations of the British during its course, Britons of this generation must not dwell on the treachery of disloyal men to such an extent as to forget the sacrifices made by large bodies of loyal Indians who helped to quell the revolt.

30. *Two Months in Arrah in 1857*, by John James Halls, p. 67.

Of the gallantry displayed by Indians while aiding the British in pre-Mutiny days not much can be related here for lack of space. To mention but one instance:

During the Chinese War of 1840, the 3rd company of the 37th Native Infantry had a brush with the Celestials which, while nearly costing all of them their lives, won them undying renown as valorous warriors. It was suddenly realized, at the close of a day's hard fighting, that this company was missing. At once two companies of Marines were despatched to hunt for them. They hurried back over the muddy ground to the scene of the day's battle. Night had fallen, and it was raining. After tramping about aimlessly for several hours they finally heard shots in the distance, and some faint hurrahs. Following the direction of these sounds, they came upon a force of Chinamen several thousand strong, who fled at their approach.

It was discovered that the missing Indians

were drawn up in a hollow square in the centre of a rice field. Up to the time of their relief they had been surrounded by the enemy, but had decided to die fighting rather than surrender. In the darkness of the cloudy, rainy day, they had become separated from their regiment. Suddenly they found themselves assailed from the rear by a large body of Chinese armed with all sorts of queer weapons. One of the sepoys was struck with a long spear and dragged out of the line. His musket was snatched from his hand, but he continued to fight with his bayonet until he was cut down.

The Indians at once formed a hollow square, and an Ensign and half a dozen men who had sprung forward to try to save the life of their unfortunate comrade succeeded in returning to their companions. A Chinaman grabbed the dead man's gun, rested it in the branch of a bush, and fired point blank at the Ensign. The Indians tried to defend themselves with their muskets, but were dismayed to find that owing to the heavy rain they could not ignite their powder with the flint and steel. Their short bayonets were no match for the long spears with which the Chinese were armed.

Finally the sepoys managed to retire to a stronger position. The rain, meanwhile, had stopped long enough to make it possible for them to use their muskets. Some of them tore the linings from their caps, drew the wet cartridges from their muskets, and cleaned the barrels by baling water into them with their hands. Thus they were enabled to fire a number of volleys at the enemy, who were less than fifty feet distant. The cowardly Chinese were driven back by the fire, and the Sepoys managed to make their way in the direction of the camp.

But the rain again descended in torrents, putting the fire-arms once more out of commission. The Chinese took advantage of this circumstance and the Sepoys were forced, for the third time, to form a hollow square. They had made up their minds to remain in this formation all night, if necessary, fighting for their lives, when the Marines came along and put the Celestials to flight. The rescuers reached them at the psychological moment, for the Chinese had managed to mount a small gun on a hill near-by and opened fire on them just as the relief party arrived. They must have been mowed down in a short time.[31]

The Indian fighter's devotion to his British General, and his spirit of self-sacrifice, is shown by an incident that occurred in the early days of the Honourable East India Company. When, in 1752, Lord Clive was hard pressed by an overwhelming number of foes, his Indian soldiers devised a means of overcoming the difficulty occasioned by shortness of rations. He was told that the white soldiers might eat the rice, while they themselves would subsist upon the water in which the cereal had been boiled.

31. *Narrative of the Expedition to China*, by Commander J. Elliot Bingham, R.N., Vol. II., pp. 237—240.

Lord Macaulay, in his *Essay on Clive*, has made this incident live in the following words:—

"During fifty days the siege (of Arcot) went on. During fifty days the young captain (Clive) maintained the defence with a firmness, vigilance, and ability which would have done honour to the oldest marshal in Europe. . . . The garrison began to feel the pressure of hunger. Under such circumstances, any troops so scantily provided with officers might have been expected to show signs of insubordination . . . But the devotion of the little band to its chief surpassed anything that is related of the Tenth Legion of Cæsar, or of the Old Guard of Napoleon. The sepoys came to Clive, not to complain of their scanty fare, but to propose that all the grain should be given to the Europeans, who required more nourishment than the natives of Asia. The thin gruel, they said, which was strained away from the rice would suffice for themselves. History contains no more touching instance of military fidelity . . ."[32]

Sacrifices such as these helped to win the battles, which have laid the foundation of British suzerainty in India.

32. Macaulay's *Essay on Clive.* Blackie's English Texts. Edited by W. H. D. Rouse, Litt.D., p. 23.

CHAPTER V.

Past Services to Britain.

FROM the earliest days of the Honourable East India Company, the soldiers of Hindostan have fought in defence of British interests. It is freely acknowledged by all authorities that Indians troops rendered important services in conquering India for Great Britain. Instances could be cited by the score to establish this point, but since it is readily admitted by all, and no authority, no matter how prejudiced he may have been against Indians, has ever questioned the importance of the part played by them in this respect, it is unnecessary to burden this book with quotations. I cannot, however, resist the temptation to reproduce some words from page 338 of the *Imperial Gazetteer of India (The*

Indian Empire), Vol. IV., wherein, while dealing with the causes of the Indian Mutiny, it is stated:

> "The Sepoy Army had built up the fabric of the British Empire in India; . . ."

Limitations of space make it impossible to recount here how Indian soldiers have helped the British to conquer various portions of India. Nor is there room for a description of how the ready, enthusiastic, and efficient aid of Rajas and Indian soldiers helped to save the British dominion in India from being wrecked by the Sepoys who mutinied in 1857. In the words of Capt. Lionel J. Trotter: but for the help of the "Sikh, Hindu and Mohammadan Sepoys and police . . our own countrymen would have fought in vain."[1] A rapid survey, however, may be made of the important campaigns in which Indians have been employed outside Hindostan proper (con-

1. *India under Victoria*, by Captain Lionel J. Trotter, Vol. II., p. 89. Similar references occur in other authentic annals of this period.

Photo by G. T. Jones & Son, Kingston-on-Thames.

SOME OF THE OFFICERS AND SOLDIERS BELONGING TO THE 23RD SIKH PIONEERS.

Composed of *Mazbi* and *Ramdasia* Sikhs.

sidering Burma as foreign territory) since the eighteenth century.

As far back as 1762 Indian soldiers were required for active service abroad. In that year the Government of Madras recruited two thousand Sepoys for an expedition to Manila. A General Order dated 20th July, 1762, directed the Major of Brigade "to bring a return to the Adjutant-General of the number of Sepoys already entered for the expedition," etc.[2] Details of this campaign are given by Maj.-Gen. Sir J. Malcolm, G.C.B., on page 330 of the Report from Select Committee on the Affairs of the East India Company, Military, printed for the House of Commons on August 16th, 1832.

Seventeen years later, on 5th October,

2. Copy of Minutes of the Most Noble the Marquis of Tweeddale, K.T., Governor and Commander-in-Chief of Madras, of the 6th day of March, 1845, and of the 28th day of March, 1845, upon the System under which Native Troops of that Presidency are employed on Foreign Service. Ordered by the House of Commons to be printed 4th April, 1867. East India (Native Troops), 191 (mentioned hereafter as *Minutes by the Marquis of Tweeddale*), p. 1.

1779, the Madras Government again called for Indian volunteers, this time to go to Bencoolan, Sumatra. A bounty of forty rupees was offered to each man who was willing to serve there for three years.[3]

On 29th April, 1794, the Madras Government directed that three temporary battalions of ten companies each should be at once brigaded for the expedition to Amboyna, one of the Molucca islands, in the Malay Archipelago. It was distinctly promised by the Commander of the Army that the "minutest attention would be given to provide for the subsistence and comfort of the families left with each corps during the absence of the troops." So ready and whole-hearted was the response that it was impossible to make use of all the Indians who immediately offered their services. This so pleased the Commander-in-Chief that he issued orders that "to reward, so far as present circumstances will permit, the merit of those Native commis-

3. *Ibid.*, p. 1.

sioned and non-commissioned officers who so gallantly offered themselves as volunteers for foreign service," they should be removed, with one step of rank each, into certain new corps which were being raised at the time.[4]

When, in 1796, it became necessary to strengthen the troops at Amboyna and Banda, these new battalions, strengthened by a draft from the 11th Battalion, were sent to the front. The reinforcements consisted of "at least a subaltern's party of artillery, two companies of European infantry, and about four of Native infantry," each company of Indian foot "complete to the fixed establishment of 68 privates, etc., and two European subalterns." The wish was expressed that the force should be composed of volunteers. Again many more than the required number instantly responded to the call. After capturing the Dutch Settlements, the troops remained until 1801 in garrison at Malacca,

4. *Ibid.*, pp. 1, 2.

Amboyna, and Banda, with only partial relief.[5]

Soon after the expedition had been sent to Amboyna, in 1794 and 1795, three entire battalions of Indian soldiers were sent to Ceylon, where they performed garrison duty at Colombo, Jaffuspatam, and Trincomalee. Two of them, the 1st and 9th Regiments of Native Infantry, remained in Ceylon until the middle of 1797. The 7th Regiment did not return until the spring of 1802.[6]

In 1797 a portion of the 3rd and 5th Native Infantry, together with the 33rd and 34th Battalions, and a detachment of the 1st, 2nd, 3rd, and 4th Native Cavalry formed an expeditionary force intended for Manila. They only proceeded as far as Penang, however, at which point in their journey the venture was abandoned. However, all the Indian ranks were granted honorary badges for the service.[7]

On 19th March, 1797, the Governor-in-

5. *Ibid.*, p. 3. 6. *Ibid.*, p. 3. 7. *Ibid.*, p. 3.

Council issued a General Order announcing that a donation of three months' family money was to be made to the heirs of all Sepoys who might be killed or die on service to "the eastward"; that a donation of two months' family allowance was to be made to the heirs of all who might die or be killed on Ceylon service; and that ten supernumerary boys were to "be allowed to each battalion, to be chosen exclusively from the near relatives of those who may have died on the service." By subsequent orders, each sepoy was allowed a "cumly" and one month's advance of pay; each battalion was allowed to take fifty boys with it, and families were allowed, whenever they might desire it, rice equal to the amount of their certificates.[8] It had been previously ordered[9] that the troops were to be given rations consisting of rice, pulses, *ghee* (clarified butter), curry condiments, salt fish, betel, and tobacco, while on board ship and on shore, during foreign service.

8. *Ibid.*, p. 4. 9. *Ibid.*, p. 3.

A small detail consisting of twenty-five of all ranks of the Body Guard with about half a hundred of the Bombay Infantry was despatched to Persia in 1800 as an escort to the British Envoy.[10]

In the initial year of the 19th century, a contingent of 5,000 troops was sent to Egypt by the East India Company to fight for his Britannic Majesty. This expedition was meant to be directed against the French, against whom Indians had valiantly fought on their own soil. Strangely enough, just a little more than a century later, Indians were convoyed farther west to France to fight side by side with the Republic's forces to keep the German hordes from despoiling the land of *liberté, égalité, fraternité.*

The Indian soldiers who were taken over to Egypt in 1801 really belonged to a force which the East India Company had got ready to send to conquer Java and the Mauritius. The Bengal detachment had reached Trin-

10. *Ibid.*, p. 4.

comalee, Ceylon, bound on this mission, when Lord Wellesley decided to divert it to Egypt to help the Army of Great Britain to expel the French from the Nile-country. The force included an experimental troop of Horse Artillery, a detachment of Foot Artillery, and a regiment of Indian Infantry volunteers.

This expedition, commanded by Sir Ralph Abercromby, sailed from Bombay. Unfortunately, one mishap after another checked its advance. First two of the transports were wrecked, and others were badly damaged during a storm while in the Red Sea. Again, the wind blew perversely from the wrong quarter, making it impossible for the troops to be landed at Suez, as had been originally planned, and detachments of them were put ashore at Kossier in May and June, 1801. They were forced to make a long march across the desert from Kossier to Keneh, suffering many hardships on the way. Thence they made their way down the left bank of the Nile to Girgeh, where they embarked in boats and were taken to Cairo. They remained there three weeks, and, on August 28th, again started down the river in boats, reaching Rosetta on the third day. To their great disgust they learned, on landing, that Alexandria, the last French stronghold, had capitulated. Thus all chance for them to fight was gone. They became a part of the British Army of Occupation for a few months, and, in July and August, 1802, set their faces towards India.[11]

A detachment of Cavalry, Artillery, Horse Artillery, and Pioneers composed of volunteers from various regiments embarked, in 1808, for service in Persia. The three battalions of Indian infantry at the time stationed at Wallajahbad, thinking that foot soldiers were to be sent on this expedition, volunteered to a man. The detachment originally intended to be despatched for service in Persia at this time consisted of 1,000 men of

11. *A Sketch of the Services of the Bengal Native Army*, by F. G. Cardew, pp. 74, 75.

all ranks. They embarked at Mangalore and disembarked at Bombay, camping there for five months. From that point the bulk of the troops were ordered back to Madras, only a small detail actually proceeding to Persia. The soldiers who returned to Madras were given a month's extra allowance and honorary badges "as a mark of distinction, and as a proof of the sense entertained by the Government of their attachment to the service, and of their meritorious conduct while absent from their own establishment."[12]

In 1810 the Government contemplated employing a portion of the Indian troops of the Madras Army in Java, and called for volunteers for "an expedition to the eastward," holding out inducements to all ranks. Seven thousand men immediately volunteered. Subsequently it was decided to give up the idea of invading Java. But the volunteers remained embodied, and later became the Madras Rifle Corps, which was

12. *Minutes by the Marquis of Tweeddale*, p. 4.

sent along with the expedition to the French Islands in 1810.[13]

Two battalions of Indian troops were ordered to Ceylon in 1818. They remained there in garrison at different stations throughout that year and during part of 1819.[14]

Six years later Indians were employed to wage war upon the King of Burma, whose soldiers had committed depredations on the eastern frontier of the East India Company's dominions. The First Burma War—as it was called—began in 1824 and ended in 1826, and resulted in the annexation by the British of Assam, Arakan, and Tenasserim, at a cost of almost 20,000 soldiers and £14,000,000. The regiments in Ava suffered terribly during the whole of their first year's service. The Sepoys were exposed to the worst possible privations of every sort. For one thing, no fresh meat was obtainable, and the Indian soldiers were compelled to subsist upon the ordinary sea rations of salt fish, etc. This

13. *Ibid.*, pp. 4, 5. 14. *Ibid.*, p. 5.

caused much sickness and mortality. Besides, the climate and the inclemency of the weather were very trying. In 1824 and 1825, out of a force of about 15,000 soldiers, 1,184 had died and about 800 had been invalided to the sea coast.

It is noteworthy that the first reinforcements that were sent to the corps to take the place of the sick and dead men were recruited at Wallajahbad, where a hospital had been established for the Indian soldiers. Although these recruits constantly witnessed the most harrowing sights, saw the Indian soldiers being brought in sick and wounded, and knew full well the privations to which they were bound to be exposed, yet they were perfectly willing to offer their services to the British in their hour of need, and nearly 2,000 embarked in successive detachments.[15]

It may be prominently mentioned here that, in spite of the fact that the regular Indian troops were given the option of accompanying

15. *Ibid.*, pp. 5—7.

their corps on foreign service, with the assurance "that any individuals unwilling, from prejudices of caste, family connections, or other good cause, to follow their colours, would be drafted into other corps," and "that no disapprobation would attach to them for such choice," they never hesitated to go to any point at any time it was intimated that they could be of service to the East India Company or to his Britannic Majesty, and finally the option was discontinued, as no advantage was taken of it.[16]

Following the campaign in Ava, Indian soldiers continued to be employed on foreign service in the Tenasserim Provinces, the Straits of Malacca, China, and Aden. Their eagerness to serve in foreign lands is demonstrated by the fact that many of the corps went abroad, on active service, again and again. In the early days, according to the Marquis of Tweeddale, K.T., Governor and Commander-in-Chief of Madras, volunteers

16. *Ibid.*, p. 5.

were actually "known to hurry down from a distance by forced marches, lest they should not be in time for embarkation."[17]

The first Afghan War (1839-1842), brought about by the meddling of Lord Auckland, then Viceroy and Governor-General of India, with the politics of Afghanistan, once again led to the employment of Indian troops. Owing to treachery, disaster after disaster befell the invading army. Most of the British and Indian soldiers were killed or died of disease, misadventure, or exposure, and the survivors suffered terrible privations. The avenging army, however, pushed into the heart of Afghanistan, British prisoners were rescued, the Afghans duly punished, and the conquering Army returned to India in triumph. Lord Ellenborough, who, in the meantime, had become Governor-General, rewarded the sepoys with their favourite sweetmeat.[18]

17. *Ibid.*, pp. 10, 11.

18. *Sketch of the Services of the Bengal Native Army*, pp. 167—192; also all histories dealing with this period.

Meanwhile, Indian troops had been conveyed to China to punish the Celestials for destroying British property (mostly opium sent from India), valued at two and a half million pounds, and insulting British officials. The first detachment, consisting mostly of Madrasi troops, sailed from Calcutta in April, 1840. They occupied the Island of Chusan on July 5th of that year, remaining there during the rest of the year, suffering from the ravages of disease throughout their stay. In January, 1841, the Island of Chuenpee, in the Canton river, was attacked. Subsequently, engagements took place at various points. The British force, meantime, moved from Canton to Hong Kong, still hard hit by epidemics of one kind or another. Some of the soldiers returned to India, those who remained in China taking part in various actions up to the latter part of the summer of 1841, and eventually embarked for the homeland in the early spring of 1842. Their place was taken by a new battalion of Indian volunteers from Bengal, who, reaching China in June, 1842, joined the forces that were at that time preparing to advance to the Yang-tse-Kiang, and in July took Chin-Kiang-Foo by storm. In this engagement three companies of Indian fighters were the first to enter into conflict with the Chinese, scattering them, and killing many of them. The British Force then prepared to advance on Nanking, but before that place could be taken, peace was concluded, and the Indians were sent back home.[19]

The second Burma War, which was brought about by the Burmese grossly maltreating British residents in Burma, once again necessitated the employment of Indian troops. Lord Dalhousie (Governor-General from 1848 to 1856) sent a deputation to the King of Burma to protest against what had happened. He issued an ultimatum on Feb. 12th, 1852, and while he was making military

19. *Ibid.*, pp. 193—195; also *Minutes of the Marquis of Tweeddale*, and many other authorities.

preparations, the Burmese fired on the flag of truce, and invaded and seized Martaban. Peace was not proclaimed until 30th June of the following year, when Pegu was annexed.

In 1858 Indian troops were taken for the second time to China. It was remarkable that these soldiers should have volunteered for service across the sea while their comrades were taking an active part in the Sepoy Mutiny then raging. The Indians, along with British and French troops, fought the Celestials, whose policy of absolutely excluding Europeans had led to this campaign. Brownlow's Punjabis were the first, either of the French or English Forces, to enter Peking, and plant the British colours on its walls in 1860.[20] The last of the Indian soldiers did not return to Hindustan until 1862.

The campaigns against the Khudu Khels of the North-West Frontier, in 1858, the

20. *History of the 20th (Duke of Cambridge's Own) Infantry (Brownlow's Punjabis)*, p. 16.

Abors of the North-East Frontier in 1858-59, and the Waziris in 1859 and 1860; the operations in the Khasiah and Jiantiah Hills in eastern India in 1862-63; the expedition to Ambela on the North-West Frontier; the war in Bhutan, in northern India in 1864-66; the campaign against the Bizoti Urakzais in 1868; the Expedition to the Black Mountain in Hazara in 1868; the second expedition against the Bizoti Urakzais in 1869; the Lushai expedition in 1871-72; the punitive measures against the Dawaris in 1872; the campaign against the Daphlas, savage tribes inhabiting the hills of Lower Assam in 1874-75; and the Naga Hills expedition in the same year, all needed large or small detachments of Indian soldiers to punish the raiding and fanatical frontiersmen, and protect life and property in the British territory which marched with other dominions.[21]

21. *Sketch of the Services of the Bengal Native Army*, pp. 290—323; and many other works.

In 1867-68 Indian fighters were required to cross the seas, to battle with the army of King Theodore of Abyssinia, who had insulted the British representative at his Court and wantonly imprisoned British subjects. Some 14,000 Indians marched for several hundred miles through a country absolutely unknown to them, from the coast to the hostile potentate's capital, Magdala, known to be strongly defended. Most of them were forced to carry their own kits all the way, while all suffered from lack of sufficient water and food. But they did not return home until they had accomplished the object for which they had been taken to Abyssinia.[22]

Indian troops went to the Malay Straits Settlement in 1875-76, to assist in putting down the insurrection at Perak, in which the Resident, Mr. Birch, had been killed.[23]

They were employed in many operations

22. *Ibid.*, pp. 316—318; also *Historical Records of the 127th Baluch Light Infantry*, pp. 15—19.

23. *Sketch of the Services of the Bengal Native Army*, p. 323; also parliamentary papers, etc.

against the frontiersmen during the following years, of which the expedition against the Jowaki Afridis in 1877, the punishment of the Naga Hill tribes in 1877-78, and the campaign against the Ranizais, in Skakot, and the Utman (or Usman) Khels in Swat, in the last-named year, may be mentioned.[24]

The second Afghan War, declared on November 21st, 1877, by Lord Lytton, then Viceroy and Governor-General, in order to drive Russian influence out of the capital of the Amir, and compel him to "consent to receive a permanent British mission within his territory," and apologize for "past transgressions," saw Indian soldiers, in three columns, headed by the late Lord (then Lt.-Gen. Sir F. S.) Roberts, Sir Donald Stewart, and Sir Samuel Browne, march upon the territories of his Highness—as he was then styled—from three different directions. In the course of this campaign, in the latter part of 1880, Lord Roberts carried out his brilliant

24. *Ibid.*, pp. 325, 326.

coup to relieve the British garrison at Kandahar, by marching his 10,000 soldiers (over 7,000 of whom were Indians) a distance of 310 miles in twenty days, over the roughest kind of country imaginable.[25]

While the Afghan war was in progress, a detachment of Indian troops was, on April 17th, 1878, despatched to the Mediterranean, under instructions from the Secretary of State for India, to be in readiness in case the advance of Russians on Constantinople in the Russo-Turkish war should assume a dangerous aspect. The force consisted of two field batteries of Royal Artillery, two regiments of Indian Cavalry, six regiments of Indian Infantry, and four companies of Sappers and Miners, mostly Sikhs, Gurkhas, and Moslems. The expeditionary troops arrived at Malta in May, 1878, and were inspected by His Royal Highness the Duke of Cambridge, Commanding-in-Chief. The Indian soldiers

25. *Ibid.*, pp. 336—374; also *Forty-one Years in India*, by Field-Marshal Lord Roberts, Vol. II., pp. 86—375.

Photo by G. T. Jones & Son, Kingston-on-Thames.

A PORTION OF THE VICEROY'S BODYGUARD SCIONS OF MANY FIGHTING CLANS.

remained at Malta for two months, and then were moved to Cyprus, from which island they were finally sent back to India towards the end of August.[26]

The outrages committed by the Mahsud Waziris, on the North-West Frontier, in 1881, determined the Government of India to send another expedition, largely composed of Indians, against these troublesome tribesmen, to punish them for their obstreperousness.[27]

The defence of Imperial interests in Egypt required the assistance of Indian troops in 1882, and they set out once again for the Nile Land. They bore the brunt of the fighting in this campaign, and completely crushed the insurrection among the African troops. On the completion of the campaign, which lasted about three months, the force returned home.[28]

26. *Sketch of the Services of the Bengal Native Army*, pp. 326, 327; also Hansard, etc.

27. *Ibid.*, pp. 375, 376; also *Regimental History of the 32nd Sikh Pioneers*, Vol. I., pp. 97—99.

28. *Sketch of the Services of the Bengal Native Army*, pp. 378—380.

Early in 1885 it was necessary to send another Indian expedition to Egypt to assist the British troops at Suakin.[29]

In the same year, Indian troops crossed over to Burma to take part in the third and last Burmese war. It was not over until 1887, when Upper Burma was annexed, and the Shan States came under the protection of the British.[30]

Tibetan aggression on the trade routes in Sikkim, and the virtual agreement of the ruler of that buffer State to become the feudatory of the Lama of Tibet, led Lord Dufferin, then Viceroy and Governor-General of India, to send, in 1888, an expeditionary force, largely Indian in composition, to enforce his ultimatum to the Chinese, Tibetan and Sikkim authorities.[31] The force did its work so well that since then there has been no trouble in Sikkim, and the Maharaja of that State is now

29. *Ibid.*, pp. 381—384.

30. *Ibid.*, pp. 384—392.

31. *Ibid.*, pp. 393, 394; also *Regimental History of the 32nd Sikh Pioneers*, Vol. I., pp. 111—135.

as loyal as loyal can be to the British Government.

A number of frontier operations next engaged the Indian troops. Of these, the Manipur campaign in 1891, and the Black Mountain expedition of the same year; the relief of Chitral in 1895; and the expedition against the Mohmund Waziris, and the Tirah campaign, of 1897 and 1898, were the most important. Some of these were very big operations, the last employing 40,000 troops.[32]

Special mention needs to be made of the fact that during the Tirah Campaign the Rajas, who theretofore had been allowed only to contribute forces, were permitted to take an active part in the fighting. His Highness the late Maharaja of Patiala (Sir Rajindra Singh Bahadur, G.C.S.I.); his Highness the late Maharaja of Cooch Behar (Sir Nripendra Narayan Bhup Bahadur, G.C.I.E., C.B.), and

32. *Ibid.*, Vol. I., pp. 139—175; also *Sketch of the Services of the Bengal Native Army*, pp. 415—427; also *History of the Imperial Service Troops of Native States*, by Brigadier General Stuart Beatson, C.B., pp. 138—152.

his Highness the Maharaja of Idar (Sir Partab Singhji, now Regent of Jodhpur), were at the front.

Sir Partab Singhji was wounded in the hand while asleep. So shy was he that for several days he told no one about his trouble, quietly keeping his hand wrapped up in a handkerchief. Not until he was threatened with blood poisoning would he allow a surgeon to bandage it properly.[33]

The call came to the Indian soldiers to help quell the mutiny that broke out among the Soudanese troops in the employ of the Uganda Protectorate, British East Africa, in 1896-7.[34]

The outbreak of the Boxer Rebellion necessitated the despatch of a large number of troops from India to put down the rising. In all, about 15,000 soldiers from Hindostan took part in this campaign in China. Of these,

33. *Ibid.*, pp., 147—152; also *The Indian Frontier War*, by Lionel James, pp. 91 *et seq.*

34. *Historical Records of the 127th Baluch Light Infantry*, pp. 105—139; also Blue Book, *Africa No. 1, 1899*.

fully 14,371 were Indians. It may be noted that this number does not include the Indians who, as an integral part of the Hong Kong garrison, took part in the fighting.[35]

It may also be noted that three of the Rajas, namely, his Highness the Maharaja of Gwalior (Sir Madho Rao Sindhia), his Highness the Maharaja of Bikaner (Sir Ganga Singh Bahadur), and his Highness the Maharaja of Idar (Sir Partab Singhji), served actively during these operations. The Maharaja of Gwalior fitted up a hospital ship. The Ruler of Bikanir took his camel corps. Sir Partab Singhji led the Jodhpur Imperial Service Troops. The Maharaja of Bikaner showed his spirit of *camaraderie* in this campaign by directing his Camel Corps to pitch the tents for the American contingent, which arrived in China so tired that it was an act of charity to do their work for them.[36]

35. *Parliamentary White Paper,* ordered by the House of Commons to be printed, March 27th, 1905.

36. *The Royal Tour in India, 1905,* by Stanley Reed, p. 116.

Trouble in Somaliland in 1903 led to soldiers being requisitioned from India.[37] By 1904 the Somali uprising had been put down; but not all the Indian fighters were sent back home. Since then there have frequently been great or small operations which have made it necessary to take fresh Indian troops there from Hindostan. Reference has been made in Chapter III. to the present strength of the Indian force in Somaliland.

Indian soldiers formed the bulk of the military escort of 3,000 troops which accompanied Captain (now Sir) Francis Edward Younghusband, who was sent by Lord Curzon, Viceroy and Governor-General, in 1904, on a mission to negotiate a treaty with the Tibetan authorities. The plucky Indians braved the rigours of the frigid climate of the "roof of the world," climbed jagged hills and precipitous mountains, and valiantly fought the Tibetans, who, badly armed though they were, had entrenched themselves in positions

37. *Parliamentary White Paper*, March 27th, 1905.

of natural vantage. According to official reports, the average altitude at which hostilities were carried on was 14,000 feet, though some battles took place at an elevation of 18,000 feet. The weather, even in midsummer, was "very inclement," and during the winter "50 degrees of frost were not unusual," and gales and storms were frequent. Besides the thirty-seven killed and 165 wounded in action, 411 died through exposure, and 671 were invalided for the same cause, but the majority of the Indians stood the severity of the climate exceptionally well. They finally forced upon the Dlai Lama the terms of the treaty so dear to the heart of Lord Curzon.[38]

This rapid survey of the campaigns in which Indians have been engaged for Britain out of the Peninsula proper does not pretend to be exhaustive. On the contrary, I am aware that many expeditions that well might have been named have been omitted. For instance, military escorts which accompanied

38. *Moral and Material Progress, 1911-12*, p. 332.

the commissions appointed for exploring and delimitating boundaries in Afghanistan in 1884, Pamir in 1895, and Aden in 1903; and a number of expeditions for the relief of garrisons stationed in out-of-the-way places on the North-West Frontier, and for punishing frontier raiders and keeping peace and order on the borders, have found no place in the chronicle. Nor have I alluded to the military and naval operations in the Persian Gulf, to suppress the smuggling of arms into the North-West Frontier. The small compass of space and the shortness of time at my disposal make it impossible for me to enumerate even all of the important expeditions in which Indians have taken part.

However, this much may be said: for many, many decades Britain has not been engaged in any fight in which Indians in large or small numbers, or British soldiers temporarily in the pay of Hindostan have not fought—and always fought bravely—on Britain's side.

The one occasion in recent years on which Indian troops did not fight side by side with British soldiers was the Boer war of 1900-1901. However, British troops numbering 8,215 were taken from the Indian garrison. It must be clearly stated that though belonging to the British Army, these men, while in India, were paid for by Hindostan, and when the call came to them they were employed by India, and in sparing them to fight in South Africa the Dependency rendered important help to the Empire.

German gossip has it that the man who in 1914 plunged most of the civilized world into war blocked Britain when it was considering the advisability of employing Indian soldiers during the Boer campaign. The Kaiser, it is declared, objected to brown men fighting white soldiers. How far this is true, I must leave for others to decide. But this much I can assert with confidence, that Indians were anxious to meet the Boers as on many other occasions they had met the other enemies of Britain. The Viceroy and Governor-General of India at that time, Lord Curzon, actually proposed to the British Cabinet, headed by Mr. Balfour, to make use of Indian cavalrymen on the veldt of South Africa—so similar to the plains of Hindostan.[39] But this offer was not accepted, because, it is said, Wilhelm chose to adopt a dog-in-the-manger policy. It has often occurred to me to inquire if the Kaiser was anxious to establish a precedent which would debar Britain from employing Indians to fight Germans should a conflict arise between the two in the future—since one day it was certain to occur.

Some of the Rajas were so loyal to the British that though naturally incensed at the Imperial authorities for giving way to racial prejudices in the matter, they ignored the hurt that had been inflicted upon their personal feelings and dignity and rendered the only

39 *India under Curzon and After*, by Lovat Fraser, p. 413

help possible in the circumstances, that of supplying a hospital ship, remounts, stores, etc. Indian medical men, among them Dr. Ranadé of Bombay, went over from the Peninsula, and Indians in South Africa, under the leadership of Mr. M. K. Gandhi, Barrister at Law, organised themselves into an Army Bearer Corps. It was touching that men of high caste and station in life should brush aside their pride of race and standing, and work in the humble capacity of coolies. But as more than one Indian who was thus employed has said to me, they cheerfully carried the wounded British soldiers from the field to the hospitals as their contribution towards Britain's success.

The Indian's attitude throughout the campaigns in which he has been engaged has ever been the same—to do, without hesitance or question, whatever duty has been apportioned, be it great or small, dangerous or otherwise. He has never stopped to theorize about the cause for which he was required to fight, but has unquestioningly obeyed the call to arms. Whether made to bear the brunt of the battle, or occupying a humble position in the fighting line, he has done his best. When denied the privilege of fighting, and merely told off to do garrison duty, he has shown no chagrin.

Such is the morale of India's fighters!

Who can compute the amount of blood that Indians have willingly—aye, eagerly—shed for Britain? But some idea of how Indians who are covered with scars from wounds go on fighting from campaign to campaign can be gained from the case of *Subadar*-Major Maula Dad Khan, C.I.E., who was called "Brave as a Lion." He originally enlisted in 1847, and retired in 1890 on a rather liberal pension granted by the Government of India. He died about six months after retiring. He was five feet nine and one-half inches high, and had a thirty-six inch chest measurement. His figure was wiry and upright, and his face was wrinkled and worn. His actual wounds were described as: "left biceps, side, back, right leg, face and right knee." He was thrice wounded seriously; was three times rewarded for conspicuous heroism; and saw about 600 of his comrades mortally or otherwise shot.[40]

40. *Historical Records of the 20th Infantry*, pp. 111, 112.

CHAPTER VI.

British Authorities on Indian Gallantry.

THROUGHOUT the long series of decades during which Indians have been fighting for Britain, both in India and elsewhere, British Generals and high civil officials have, from time to time, placed on record their appreciation of the soldierly qualities of the martial races of Hindostan. If all these complimentary statements were gathered together, they would fill many volumes. Even a fairly representative collection of them would make a large book. In the space here available, all that can be attempted is to quote a few extracts, taken hap-hazard, to give an idea of what the British officers commanding India's fighters think of them.

As far back as the early part of 1784, I

Photo by G. T. Jones & Son, Kingston-on-Thames.

SIKH LANCERS.

find the following comment of Lieutenant-General Lang, then commanding the Army, respecting the service of the Indian Cavalry:

> "The conduct of the Cavalry during the war has been such as to deserve every commendation. Owing to the smallness of their numbers and the necessity of making use of them upon every occasion, they have undergone greater fatigues than other corps in the field. They have ever cheerfully performed the services they have been employed upon, and appear entitled to every consideration from Government."[1]

By 1796 Indian troops had begun to cross the "black water" to engage in battle with Britain's foes. In a letter dated July 19th, of that year, Adjutant-General Colonel Barry Close wrote in most favourable terms of the troops employed at Amboyna. He declared:

> "The General has desired me to signify

1. *Historical Records of the 2nd Madras Lancers*, by Colonel John B. Edwards, p. 8.

the satisfaction he has experienced in perusing the desirable accounts you have given of the corps under your command since its departure from the coast, and the cheerfulness with which the men have proceeded on every service that has occurred for them in the distant quarter in which they are employed."[2]

In 1797 the Governor of Madras in Council noticed "the unexampled alacrity and spirit with which the Coast Native troops have embarked for foreign service during the war," and stated that he was "naturally led to consider every means of preserving that spirit, and of rewarding that zeal."[3]

In 1799 General Harris, in a despatch, said of the Indian soldiers:

"The Gallant behaviour of the Native Troops who were alone employed (in the campaign against Doondiah Waugh, the

2. *Minutes by the Marquis of Tweeddale*, p. 3.
3. *Ibid.*, pp. 3, 4.

freebooter of Mysore), was highly honorable to them."[4]

Captain Mundy, in his *Pen and Pencil Sketches* (pp. 59, 60), said, regarding the reviewing of Indian infantry at Agra by the Commander-in-Chief, General Lord Combermere, in 1828:

"It was impossible to avoid remarking the superiority of the sepoy over the European corps in steadiness and regularity of movement."

The Hon. Mountstuart Elphinstone, Governor of Bombay, 1819 to 1827, the famous statesman, diplomat, and scholar, who passed the best part of his life in India when it was in a disturbed state, said of the Indian soldiers:

"Their freedom from gross debauchery is the point in which the Hindus appear to most advantage. . . . If we compare them

4. *Historical Records of the 2nd Madras Lancers*, p. 28.

with our own, the absence of drunkenness, and of immodesty in their other vices, will leave the superiority in purity of manners on the side least flattering to our self-esteem."

On September 10th of the next year (1800), Colonel Wellesley, afterwards the first Duke of Wellington, reporting on the action at Conahgul, during the second campaign against Doondiah Waugh, said:

"I cannot avoid taking this opportunity of expressing my sense of the conduct of the troops. Upon this occasion their determined valour and discipline were conspicuous and their conduct and that of their Commanding Officers . . . . have deserved my most particular approbation."[5]

Sir John Malcolm, Governor of Bombay, 1827-1830, in a letter to Lord William Bentinck, dated November 27th, 1830, wrote:

"We have, through the efforts of our

5. *Ibid.*, pp. 31, 32.

Native army, triumphed in wars and rebellions. Plots and conspiracies may be formed, but they will never succeed while we maintain the good spirit and fidelity of this branch of our force. This our enemies, avowed and secret, well know; and all their efforts have been and will hereafter be directed to its corruption. This object has never been but very partially effected. . ."[6]

To this I may parenthetically add that even during the Sepoy Mutiny of 1857—the only serious disaffection among Indian fighters in British employ—a large number of Indian soldiers remained faithful, and fought to save the British from being driven out of the Peninsula; while some of them actually went to China to preserve British interests there.

In 1832 a number of military witnesses were examined before the Select Committee

6. *Reports from (Parliamentary) Committees;* 18 vols., 9. *East India Company's Affairs* . . V. Military Session, 6th December, 1831—16th August, 1832, Vol. XIII., p. 346.

of the House of Commons, which was at that time inquiring into the affairs of India, as managed by the Honourable East India Company. One of them was Sir Jasper Nicolls, later Commander-in-Chief of India. When he was asked whether the habits of the Indian soldier were orderly, and whether he was easily managed, he replied:

> "Very much so; his habits are very simple, and he is very easily managed."

Comparing the Sepoys with European soldiers, he declared:

> "I think the command of an European regiment would be more difficult than the command of a brigade of sepoys; it would be much easier to control 5,000 sepoys than it would 1,000 Europeans."[7]

At the same inquiry, Major-General Sir Thomas Reynell, speaking of the character of the sepoys, said:

7. *Ibid.*, p. 1, 2.

" . . . they are subordinate; they are patient; and they are certainly obedient to their orders. I consider them to be animated by a good spirit, and I have had a good opportunity of witnessing it in the late service before Bhurtpore. There I have seen them in the trenches working at very laborious employments, and, I believe, contrary to their own religious feelings. . . . I consider them, generally speaking, an efficient army, the Bengal army."[8]

Continuing his evidence, and in reply to the question:

"Now, as compared with the European soldier; I mean as to order and being easily managed?" Major-General Reynell said:

"I think he is much more orderly than European soldiers in general, from the mere circumstance of his not being so given to drink."[9]

Major-General Sir H. Worsley, in a letter

8. *Ibid.*, p. 18. 9. *Ibid.*, p. 18.

dated March 30th, 1832, wrote to Mr. T. Hyde Villiers:

"It will be no disparagement of any other troops to say, that hitherto the Native army of India has never been surpassed for fidelity to the Government, and attachment to their officers; nor 'yielded to those of any other nation in point of discipline and effective valour.' . . . They are . . . the most orderly, respectful and obedient soldiers in the world. . . ."[10]

In his evidence before the Select Committee on the Affairs of the East India Company, in 1832, Major-General Sir John Malcolm (who has been already quoted) gave his opinion of the Indian Artilleryman in the following words:

"The golandauze, or native artillerymen, are, in my opinion, most efficient. The artillery is a favourite service with the highest tribes of the Hindoos in India, and they

10. *Ibid.*, p. 435.

are remarkable for attaining excellence both in discipline and in gunnery. Some of the native horse artillery belonging to Madras have lately been under my orders, and they appeared to me a most efficient body of men. I have further to remark upon the native artillery, that they are of the greatest use in saving the European artillery from going upon those lesser detachments to posts at a distance from their headquarters, which have been found very materially to deteriorate their discipline, and I deem the native corps of artillery in this particular, as well as in others, a very essential one. I am not of opinion with many, that we incur any risk of a political nature by imparting such knowledge to the natives, because the natives have proved, in the corps that they have formed, that they have perfect means of becoming instructed, and instructing others in this branch of military force. The native artillery of Scindia and Holkar were not inferior, in my opinion, to any body of that class of men that we have formed."[11]

In the same Committee, Colonel Pennington, who had served in the Bengal artillery, when examined on March 12th, 1832, said, regarding Indian artillerymen:

"A part of the enemy captured at their guns were delivered over to me by Lord Lake; we at that time had not 40 men European, and we were so low that we were 11 days in the trenches without relief, and he transferred those men to me, and I had occasion to drill them a little; but when practiced to all the business of loading and firing, they were as prompt and as ready as any men. They did not at first know manœuvring, but with a little patience I soon taught them manœuvring. They were footmen, but no men ever stood better to their guns than they did. . . . . You may confide in a native artilleryman as much as

11. *Ibid.*, p. 40.

you may in an European; there are no men in whom you may put more trust."[12]

Colonel David Leighton, C.B., who had for some thirty-six years served in the Bombay Presidency, declared that the Indian artillerymen:

> " . . . save the Europeans from being detached in small bodies; they stand the climate much better, and save a number of lives of Europeans."[13]

The Marquis of Tweeddale, Commander-in-Chief, etc., describes how the 4th Regiment of the troops sent to China on the occasion of the first China War, suffered severely from sickness, but "never uttered one word of complaint, nor ever asked to be relieved." He goes on to relate:

> "With the full knowledge of all that has been suffered by their fellow-soldiers, and

12. *Ibid.*, p. 55. 13. *Ibid.*, p. 134.

after having witnessed the successive debarkations of the numerous invalids of the 4th Regiment in particular, with whom they have been in constant and immediate communication when on duty at the Presidency Hospital, the 42nd Regiment has embarked without a moment's hesitation on the same duty; and not only without a single man asking for his removal or discharge, of which all had the free option, but with the addition of a number of recruits enlisted after the order had been issued, and of several men from other corps, who exchanged into the regiment for the purpose of joining relations, including four from the 6th Regiment, Native Infantry, who had already been in China."[14]

To support his statement, he quoted an extract from a letter from Major-General D'Aguilar, dated September 23rd, 1844, which read:

14. *Minutes by the Marquis of Tweeddale*, p. 9.

"No care or consideration shall be wanting towards the sepoys who, amidst sickness as sudden in its later effects as unparalleled, have evinced throughout the most exemplary patience and good conduct."[15]

No wonder that the Marquis of Tweeddale should have spoken thus highly of the Indian soldiers.

"Altogether their character is such as has, I believe, never belonged to any other body of mercenary troops.

"It differs essentially from that of the German auxiliaries or free companies of former times in Europe, who, serving for pay, would never hesitate to take whichever side could give the highest terms. . . . Very noble proofs were . . . given by our men of fidelity to their colours, in circumstances of extreme temptation, when, in the wars with Hyder Ali and Tippoo Sooltan, constant

15. *Ibid.*, p. 9.

attempts were made to induce them to take service against us.

"They perhaps most resemble the Swiss corps, formerly in the French and other Continental services; faithful to their employers, not from any national feeling, but from having been for successive generations in their pay, and having thus become personally identified with them in all their military character.

" . . . if only the terms of his contract be faithfully fulfilled by his employers, the sepoy is found invariably true and faithful to the Government he serves."[16]

Coming down to the days of the Sepoy Mutiny, I find numerous complimentary references to the behaviour of the Indian fighters who helped to conquer the mutineers. Brigadier Hope Grant, Commanding Cavalry Division, in a despatch, dated Delhi, Sept. 17th, 1857, declared that:

16. *Ibid.*, p. 13.

"Nothing could be steadier, nothing more soldier-like, than their bearing."[17]

Major-General Sir H. Barnard, K.C.B., Commanding, issued a Field Force Order, dated Delhi, June 9th, 1857, in which he spoke of the "Queen's Own Corps of Guides" in terms of the warmest praise. He said:

"The Major-General has the gratifica- to announce to the troops the arrival in camp this day of the Guide Corps, consisting of three troops of cavalry and six companies of riflemen. This distinguished body of men, whose services on the Peshawar Frontier and in various parts of the Punjab are well known to many in this force, have marched from Mardan, in Yusufzai, to Delhi, a distance of 580 miles, in 22 days—a march of which Sir H. Barnard believes there is no parallel on record, and which reflects the very highest credit on

17. *Twelve Years of a Soldier's Life in India*, by Major W. S. R. Hodson, B.A., edited by his brother, the Rev. George H. Hodson, M.A., p. 294

Captain Daly, the Commandant, and the officers and men of the Corps. The Guides, notwithstanding their long and rapid march, are in perfect order and ready for immediate service, and the Major-General recommends these brave and loyal soldiers to the favourable notice of their comrades of the various regiments in camp."[18]

Later in the year, on November 18th, Captain G. Wardlaw, 6th Carabiniers, in a despatch written from camp Narnoul, wrote:

> " . . . I can only say that no European corps could have charged with greater spirit or more *effect* than did the Guides on this occasion. . . ."[19]

A month later, December 18th, the Guides commenced to march back to the frontier, and arrived at Mardan on February 11th, 1858. They stopped for a week at Peshawar, and on February 2nd Major-

18. *Historical Records of the Services of the Queen's Own Corps of Guides*, p. 11.
19. *Ibid.*, p. 16.

General Cotton, Commanding the Peshawar Division, ordered that the troops of the Peshawar Cantonment should be paraded under his personal command to receive and welcome the Corps of Guides on its return from the siege of Delhi. A royal salute was fired in their honour as they approached the parade ground, the troops saluted and the Major-General delivered the following address to the Guides and his own forces:

> " . . . I have invited you here as brother-soldiers of the Frontier this day, to welcome you on your return from the siege of Delhi, and to acknowledge, in the most public manner, the high sense we entertain of the value and importance of the service rendered by you to the State during the progress of the present insurrectionary war. In the name of Colonel Edwardes, our Commissioner, on my own account, and in behalf of my brother officers and soldiers, I warmly greet you on your return amongst us.

"We respect, we honour you, and we feel proud of being re-associated with men whose deeds of daring have earned our noble profession never-dying fame. . . ."[20]

A *feu de joie* with an accompanying salute of twenty-one guns followed the address.

As if this were not enough, the Honourable Court of Directors, Military Department, sent a letter to the Government of India, No. 50, dated August 30th, 1858, which read in part:

"We cannot too strongly express our entire concurrence in the sentiments expressed by Major-General Cotton in his division order on the occasion of the return of the Guides to the Frontier.

"That Corps, by the extraordinary alacrity with which they proceeded to Delhi, marching 580 miles in twenty-one days, and having during those twenty-one days turned off the road twelve miles one

20. *Ibid.*, p. 17.

night to attack mutineers, by their remarkable services before Delhi, where, for nearly four months, both officers and men were constantly in action, sometimes twice a day; by their singular fidelity as shown by the fact that of 800 men not one man deserted to the enemy, whilst 350 of them were killed and wounded, and by their heroic gallantry, having established for themselves the strongest claim to our approbation and favour. We desire that these our sentiments be conveyed to them through their gallant commander Major Daly."[21]

Most glowing, too, were the compliments bestowed upon the 2nd Punjab Infantry by Brigadier-General Walpole, Commanding the Division. He wrote, in 1858, following the siege of Lucknow:

"The Brigadier-General has much pleasure in thanking the Brigadiers, Officers, Non-Commissioned Officers, and

21. *Ibid.*, p. 17.

soldiers of the Division under his command, for their gallant behaviour in the field and for good conduct generally during the recent operations on the left bank of the Goomtee. To their soldier-like conduct and willing exertions during a time of considerable fatigue, may be attributed this success with a loss small in comparison with the results obtained; and with regiments in such an excellent state of discipline as those forming this Division, success must follow every duty they are called upon to perform."[22]

Lieutenant-Colonel Green, Commandant of the 2nd Punjab Infantry, before proceeding to Bombay on September 15th, 1858, issued a regiment order, of which the following is an extract:

"Lieutenant-Colonel Green has had the good fortune to lead the regiment in the following engagements during the campaign:

22. *History of the 2nd Punjab Infantry*, pp. 23, 24.

"The siege, assault and capture of Delhi, including the battle of Najafgarh, 'Bulandshahr, Agra, relief of the Lucknow Garrison, Cawnpore, Khudaganj, siege and capture of Lucknow, besides several minor skirmishes;' and he deems it only fair to both officers and men to say that the only fault he has had to find with them has been an occasional too great eagerness to close with the enemy.

"On no occasion has any portion of the regiment met with the slightest check, however superior in numbers the enemy might be, and it is with the greatest pride, Lieutenant-Colonel Green assures all ranks, that he ever heard the highest admiration of the regiment expressed on all sides while it was employed with the army in the field."[23]

When the Indian soldiers who had fought so bravely in the Abyssinian Campaign, 1867-8, embarked for their return to India, Sir

23. *Ibid.*, p. 27.

Robert Napier, Commander-in-Chief (afterwards Lord Napier of Magdala), personally thanked them for the good services they had rendered in this crisis. Speaking in *Hindustani*, he said:

"Native Officers and men of the Beloochees, I have called you together to tell you how greatly pleased I have been with the conduct of the regiment during the past campaign. When you came to Abyssinia you had already established your reputation as a distinguished corps, and now you have added still greater lustre to your name. I have watched you throughout your service with the Abyssinian force, and have been much gratified with the ready obedience you have always yielded to your officers.

"Whenever I have had to call on you for immediate duty, I have noticed with the utmost satisfaction the celerity with which you make ready for the work, and the energy with which you carry it out, and whenever I have called on your regiment

MOSLEM SOLDIERS.

for such duty I have felt satisfied that my wishes would be faithfully executed.

"Your work in the passes did you credit, and the steadiness with which you marched through a most difficult country proved your powers of endurance.

"When we arrived at Magdala, I was very sorry that your left wing was not with us. I missed them very much. When on the night before the storming of the fortress my attendant told me that the left wing had marched into camp, I said, 'Now all is well, my Beloochees are here.'"[24]

The versatility of the Indian soldier is proved by the report of Major Lang, R.E., Principal of the Thomason College at Rurki, on the work of the men of all ranks of the Queen's Own Corps of Guides, twenty-five in number, who had been sent, in June, 1873, to be taught to act as draughtsmen, surveyors, etc. He wrote of them, reporting

24. *Historical Records of the 127th Baluch Light Infantry*, pp. 18, 19.

to the Government of the North-West Provinces:

"Their good conduct and cheerful industry speak highly for their own character and discipline, and also for that of their Native Officer Mahmud Khan, and altogether there has not been probably in the College a class more willing to learn, pleasant to teach, and easy to manage, despite the difficulties which these men, essentially of the sword and spear, have experienced in learning the use of drawing pencils, pen, brush, and in the delicate handling of surveying instruments."[25]

On the occasion of his reviewing the Indian troops at Malta in 1878, his Royal Highness the Duke of Cambridge, Commanding-in-Chief, said:

"His Royal Highness cannot speak too highly of their soldierly qualities.

25. *Historical Records of the Services of the Queen's Own Corps of Guides*, p. 30.

Their uniform good conduct and smartness reflects the greatest credit on all ranks. Their steadiness under arms and drill and the excellent state of their camps leave nothing to be desired."[26]

Colonel C. M. Macgregor, C.B., C.S.I., C.I.E., President of the commission of enquiry at Kabul, writing in 1879, went out of his way to bestow praise upon the Guides. He wrote:

"The conduct of the escort of the Queen's Own Guides does not form part of the enquiry contrusted to the commission, but they have in the course of these enquiries had the extreme gallantry of the bearing of these men so forcibly brought to their notice that they cannot refrain from placing on record their humble tribute of admiration. They do not give their opinion hastily, but they believe that the

26. *Sketch of the Services of the Bengal Native Army*, by F. G. Cardew, pp. 326, 327.

annals of no Army and no Regiment can show a brighter record of devoted bravery than has been achieved by this small band of Guides. By their deeds they have conferred undying honour, not only on the Regiment to which they belong, but on the whole British Army."[27]

The British Resident in Kashmir wrote in 1880 regarding the good work of the 2nd Punjab Infantry at Gilgit, as follows:

> "Major Biddulph has requested me to let you know how extremely well the men of his guard from your regiment have behaved during the recent troubles at Gilgit.
>
> "On one occasion he writes:
>
> "'My men of the 2nd Punjab Infantry behaved in a manner beyond all praise, and I cannot find words to express what deserves to be said of them, not a word of impatience escaped them, though they

27. *Historical Records of the Services of the Queen's Own Corps of Guides*, p. 41.

Photos by G. T. Jones & Son, Kingston-on-Thames.

GENERAL GURNAM SINGH,
PRIME MINISTER, PATIALA STATE.

SIKH OFFICER, IMPERIAL SERVICE
TROOPS.

knew that every moment's delay might be fatal, as they picked up one sepoy after another and encouraged him to persevere, sometimes halting for ten minutes at a time to allow the wearied Cashmere Sepoys to rest.' "[28]

The Secretary of State for India, in a despatch to the Governor-General in Council, dated London, January 6th, 1881, republished in the *Gazette of India* of February 12th of the same year, commenting upon the march from Kabul to Kandahar, wrote:

"The march from Kabul to Kandahar reflects the highest credit on Lieutenant-General Sir Frederick Roberts and on the Officers, Non-Commissioned Officers and soldiers, British and Native, composing the force. (It may be noted in passing that 7,000 of the 10,000 troops were Indian).

"The rapidity with which the long

28. *History of the 2nd Punjab Infantry*, p. 42.

march was, under trying circumstances, accomplished evidences the perseverance, efficiency, discipline and spirit of the troops.

"Arrived at Kandahar, no time was lost. A successful reconnaissance in force was the precurser of an action resulting in the defeat and dispersion of the Afghan army and the capture of their guns, 32 in number.

"The professional ability, foresight and skill displayed by Lieutenant-General Sir Frederick Roberts was well seconded by the courage and perseverance of the officers and men under his command; and thus Afghanistan has again had full experience of the power, loyalty, devotion and gallantry of the army of the Queen Empress of India."[29]

Commenting upon the same campaign, Lieutenant-General Sir F. Haines, in

29. *Historical Records of the 2nd Sikh Infantry, Punjab Frontier Force*, p. 31.

General Order of the Commander-in-Chief, dated April 7th, 1881, in which he relinquished the Command in India, wrote:

> "Sir Donald Stewart's march from Kandahar to Kabul, and his brilliant battle at Ahmed Khel, and Sir Frederick Roberts' march from Kabul to Kandahar, and his equally brilliant battle there, were trials successfully overcome, of which any General and any troops might well be proud."[30]

The late Lord Roberts, commenting upon the troops he conducted to Kandahar, thus writes in *Forty-one Years in India* (Vol. II., pages 373-5):

> "I shall never forget the feeling of sadness with which I said good-bye to the men who had done so much for me. I looked upon them all, Native as well as British, as my valued friends. And well I might, for

30. *Ibid.*, p. 34.

never had a Commander been better served. From first to last a grand spirit of *camaraderie* pervaded all ranks. At the Peiwar Kotal, at Charasia, and during the fighting round Kabul, all were eager to close with the enemy, no matter how great the odds against them. Throughout the march from Kabul all seemed to be animated with but one desire, to effect, cost what it might in personal risk, fatigue, or discomfort, the speedy release of their beleaguered fellow-soldiers in Kandahar; and the unflagging energy and perseverance of my splendid troops seemed to reach their full height when they realized they were about to put forth their strength against a hitherto successful enemy. Their exemplary conduct, too, under circumstances often of the most trying nature, cannot be praised in terms too strong or too full. Notwithstanding the provocation caused by the cruel murder of any stragglers who fell into the hands of the

Afghans, not one act infringing the rules of civilized warfare was committed by my troops. The persons and property of the natives were respected, and full compensation for supplies was everywhere given. In short, the inhabitants of the districts through which we passed could not have been treated with greater consideration nor with a lighter hand had they proved themselves friendly allies; and the conduct of the troops will ever be to me as pleasing a memory as are the results which they achieved."

Most enthusiastic was the praise of Major-General Sir George White, V.C., K.C.B., regarding the services of the Beloochees during the third Burma War. He sent a letter which was read on the presentation of the medals to the regiment at Karachi on May 1st, 1889. I quote the following extract from it:

"I gladly testify that it is greatly owing to the ability and zeal of their officers, both

European and native, and to the dash and endurance of the men, that that district of Burma (Upper Burma), which was the most disturbed, is now the most quiet and settled . . . every officer and man has earned the medal by showing dash when ordered to face the enemy, and by cheerful endurance of hardship and fatigue on all occasions, when called on for an effort."[31]

Sir E. Elles, in his despatch regarding the results of the Mohmand Expedition, dated October 13th, 1897, quoted in the *Historical Records of the 20th (Duke of Cambridge's Own) Infantry, Brownlow's Punjabis*, on page 93, said:

" . . . but the splendid force under my command would, I believe, have made but little of any possible opposition. I cannot speak too highly of the 20th Punjab Infantry and the second battalion of 1st

31. *Historical Records of the 127th Baluch Light Infantry*, p. 72.

Gurkhas, on whom the brunt of the work fell. I would wish for no better regiments for hill fighting. . . ."

Ernest J. L. Berkeley, Esquire, C.B., Consul-General and Commissioner, in a letter dated from Eldòmo Ravine, March 29th, 1899, quoted on page 132 of the *Historical Records of the 127th Baluch Light Infantry*, referred in glowing terms to the work of the Indian soldiers in helping to quell the mutiny in the Uganda Protectorate in 1897-98. He wrote:

> "So far as I am aware, the 27th Bombay (Light) Infantry is the first regiment that has ever proceeded so far into the interior of Africa; both officers and men have suffered many hardships in distant parts of the Protectorate; but, despite every obstacle, the regiment has performed the task for which it was sent, with a gallantry and success to which I gladly pay this brief tribute."

No praise could be higher than that bestowed upon India's fighters by General Sir Arthur Power Palmer, K.C.B., the Commander-in-Chief of India when the East African medals and Order of Merit were presented to them at the Brigade Parade at Karachi, on November 17th, 1900, upon their return from British East Africa. He said:

> "The manner in which the Indian Army has shown itself always ready to obey the call of duty, whether in campaigns in India or beyond the seas, must impress foreign nations with the fighting resources of the British Empire."[32]

During his recent tour in India, so impressed was Frederick William, the German Crown Prince, with the Gurkhas, that he wrote on p. 120 of his book, *From My Hunting Day-Book*:

"They are small but extraordinarily wiry

32. *Ibid.*, pp. 141, 142.

and tough little people, who fear neither hell nor the devil."

In the campaign raging in Europe in 1914 the Indians engaged in the combat showed that the German Crown Prince was not wrong in forming this estimate. The Gurkhas, Sikhs, and others in the employ of the British Indian Government, and that of the Rajas (belonging to the Imperial Service Troops, etc.), fought so bravely as to elicit the following message from the British Commander-in-Chief, Field-Marshal Sir John French, to their Commander, Sir J. Willcocks:

> "Please congratulate . . . Indian troops on their gallant conduct, and express my gratitude to them."[33]

33. *The Times* (London), November 5th, 1914, p. 8, col. 2; also other London newspapers of that date.

INDEX.